Not your usual November print and go Lessons

© 2015 Lucky Jenny Publishing, Inc.
Plymouth, CA
Lucky Willy Imprint

ISBN-13: 978-0692564615
ISBN-10: 0692564616

Not Your Usual November Print and Go Lessons is published by people and mistakes happen, if you find typos or errors please email publisher@luckyjenny.com.

Classroom reproduction only.
All Rights Reserved

November Thematic No Prep for Fifth Grade

This No Prep Unit includes pintables and passages that can easily stand alone or serve as springboards for discussion and expansion. They are November and Thanksgiving themed and most are matched with video or interactive clips from Scholastic, History.com and Plimouth Plantation.

This No Prep Unit contains social studies activities, Common Core State Standards aligned English Language Arts and math lessons, art projects, school culture and hope projects, math task cards, a science experiment and an all new Wampanoag Cinderella story with an huge interactive notebook literary component to help deepen student understanding of literary elements and the Wampanoag culture.

All lessons are © Elizabeth Chapin-Pinotti

If you find any mistakes or typos, please email elizabethpinotti@gmail.com and I'll make any necessary corrections.

Borders and clip art:
https://www.teacherspayteachers.com/Store/Krista-Wallden

Fall clips:
https://www.teacherspayteachers.com/Product/Fall-Clips-by-LG-Doodles-1364170

Heart Pocket Created by Anh-Thi Tang - Tangstar Science

November Thematic No Prep for Fifth Grade

Table of Contents

November Outline and Clips to Watch Math the Printables and Lessons	page 5
#1 Wampanoag Facts Printable	page 7
#2 Wampanoag Facts Printable: Language	page 8
#3 Wampanoag Folklore Printable	page 20
My Own Wampanoag Tale	page 21
# 4 My Notebook Wampanoag Words	page 25
# 5 Before the First Thanksgiving	page 27
# 6 The First Thanksgiving	page 28
# 7 The Mayflower	page 29
# 8 The Landing	page 30
# 9 The Mayflower Compact	page 31
# 10 Plymouth Colony – What Would You Do?	page 32
# 11 My Compact	page 33
# 12 The Pilgrims	page 34
Achiq: The Wampanoag Cinderella – The Story	page 35
Achiq: The Wampanoag Cinderella – Interactive Notebook Story Unit	page 42
Thanksgiving Science: Cranberry Chemistry – Spy Ink	page 78
Turkey Glyphs	page 82
Fall Art Projects	page 86
Leaf Pressing	
Corn Husk Dolls	
Make a Mayflower	
# 15 Veteran's Day	page 86
I Am Hopeful – I Am Thankful Unit	page 89
A unit that helps students find hope in their lives as well as things to be thankful for.	
Thanksgiving Math	page 93
Hubbub	page 94
Fifth Grade Thanksgiving/November Math Task Cards	page 95

November Thematic No Prep for Fifth Grade

Clips to Match Worksheets

Discuss Wampanoag

Watch About the Wampanoag
Scholastic Video http://bcove.me/m5b5ehss

#1 Wampanoag Facts Worksheet

Explore "The First Thanksgiving" Interactive Adventure on the Plimouth Plantation Website https://www.plimoth.org/sites/default/files/media/olc/intro.html

Go Over Wampanoag Words – print Word Wall Cards beforehand. Divide students into groups and have them draw pictures to match the words. Multiple copies of each word is fine as you may post more than one word wall.

2 Wampanoag Facts Worksheet

---

3 Wampanoag Folklore Worksheet

Students may work alone or in groups to construct their own story.

Extension Activity: Make Big Books out of stories on butcher paper and share stories with each other and younger grades

---

4 My Notebook Wampanoag Words

Revisit the Wampanoag Word Wall and work on interactive notebook vocabulary

---

Read and do "The First Thanksgiving Worksheet. If there is time revisit "The Interactive Adventure" from above. If the technology is available have student pairs travel individually through the adventure.

There are great interactive resources that work well as whole class activities on Smartboards: http://www.scholastic.com/scholastic_thanksgiving/

November Thematic No Prep for Fifth Grade

Clips to Match Worksheets

#6 The First Thanksgiving: It Was Really Lincoln.

Discuss the origins of the holiday and have students complete the worksheet #6

As you watch the video clip of the Proclamation being read – help students understand the photographs and what is being said – what the words mean and why it was important for the country to give thanks.
https://www.youtube.com/watch?v=9nU8yOHQKhQ
This seems complication but students can understand.

History.com video on the Mayflower
http://www.history.com/topics/mayflower/videos/deconstructing-history-mayflower

7 The Mayflower Worksheet

History.com Video http://www.history.com/topics/mayflower

#8 The Landing Worksheet

Watch "The Mayflower Compact" on
http://www.teachertube.com/video/the-mayflower-compact-drive-thru-history-297549

#9 The Mayflower Compact

Discuss and do #10 Plymouth Colony What Would You Do?

Virtual Field Trip to Plimouth Plantation
http://www.plimoth.org/learn/just-kids/thanksgiving-virtual-field-trip

---

Discuss and complete: # 11 My Compact and #12 The Pilgrims

Do: Quick Skits – have student pair up or work in groups of three to make a two minute skit of something they have learned in November.

#1 Wampanoag Facts

Wampanoag: What does it mean?
Wampanoag means "Easterners.

The Wampanoag's were originally natives of Massachusetts and Rhode Island. It was these brave natives who befriended the pilgrims of Plimouth Plantation. They were very influential in helping the Europeans learn to adapt to the conditions of the land that was so new to them.

Sadly, disease, brought over by the settlers, and attacks by the British killed most of the Wampanoag people before the Pilgrims even arrived.

Modern World Connection: The Wampanoag tribe has its reservation on Martha's Vineyard. Reservations are lands that belong to Native American tribes and are under the tribe's exclusive control. They have their own governments. Reservations are like small countries within the United States, but the Wampanoag are also citizens of the United States. Today, there are about 300 members of the Wampanoag tribe.

Write two complete sentences that tell who the Wampanoag people are:

_____
_____
_____
_____
_____
_____
_____
_____
_____
_____
_____

#2 Wampanoag Facts

Language: Wampanoag (Massachusett)

Today, the Wampanoag's speak English. In the past, they spoke their native Wampanoag (Massachusett) language. Some modern Wampanoag are trying to bring back their language.

Look at your word wall and write five sentences using Wampanoag words and then translate your sentence.

Example: *My nitka fed aquit annum.*
            My mother fed one dog.

_____
_____
_____
_____
_____
_____
_____
_____
_____
_____
_____
_____
_____

#2 Wampanoag Facts

Language: Wamanoag (Massachusett)

Today, the Wampanoag's speak English. In the past, they spoke their native Wamanoag (Massachusett) language. Some modern Wampanoag are trying to bring back their language.

Wamanoag (Massachusett) Word Wall

dog

aunum

wolf

ontoquas

bear

maske

raccoon

ausupp

fox

whauksis

deer

ottucke

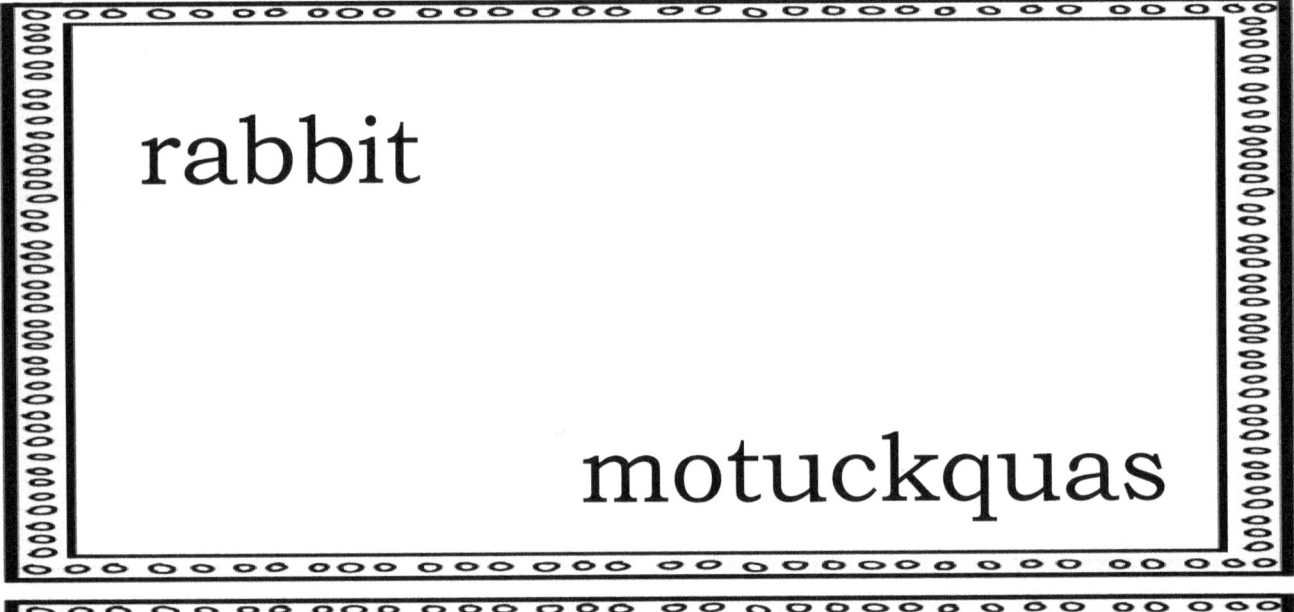

rabbit

motuckquas

squirrel

shannucke

eagle

wobsacuk

owl

wewes

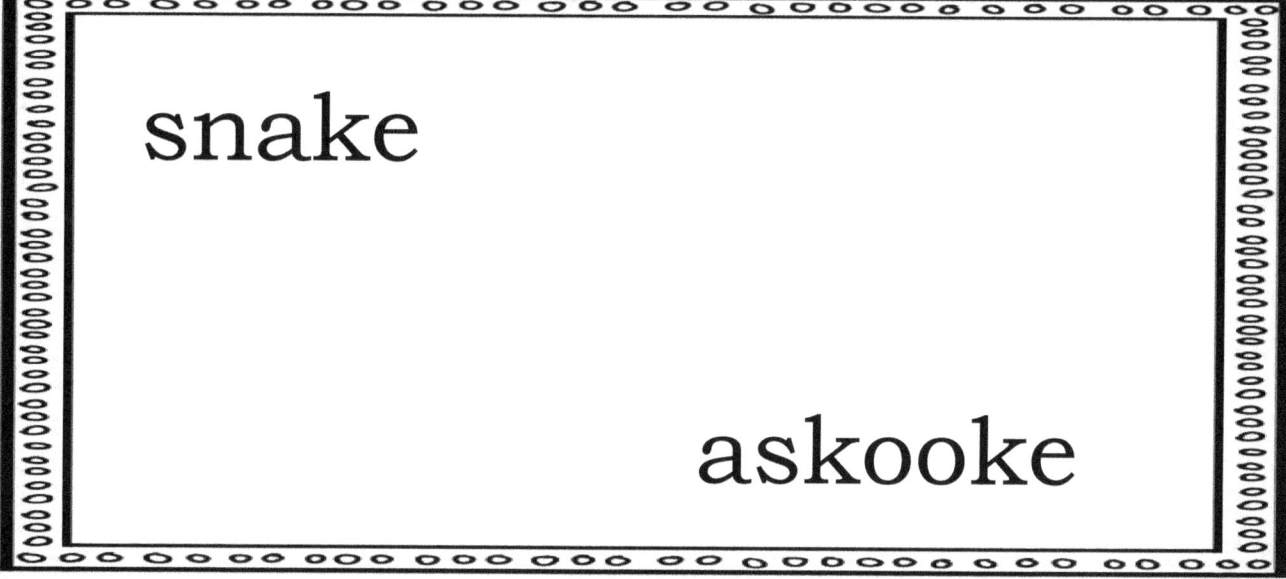

snake

askooke

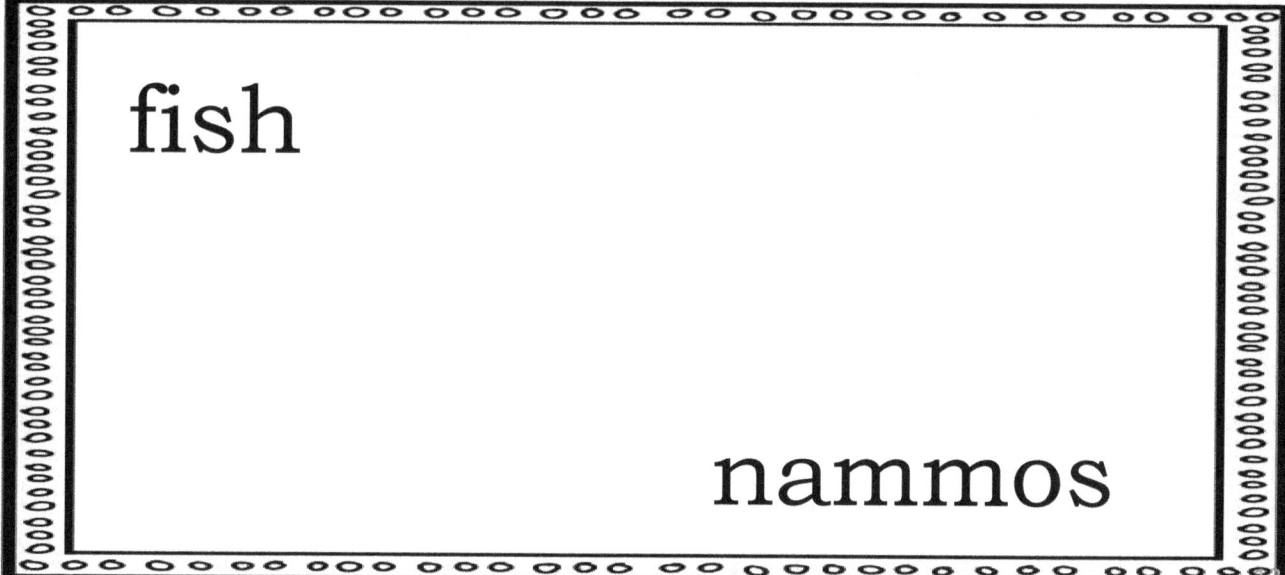

fish

nammos

| one | aquit |

| two | nees |

| three | nis |

four — yoaw

five — abbona

six — sannup

man

sannup

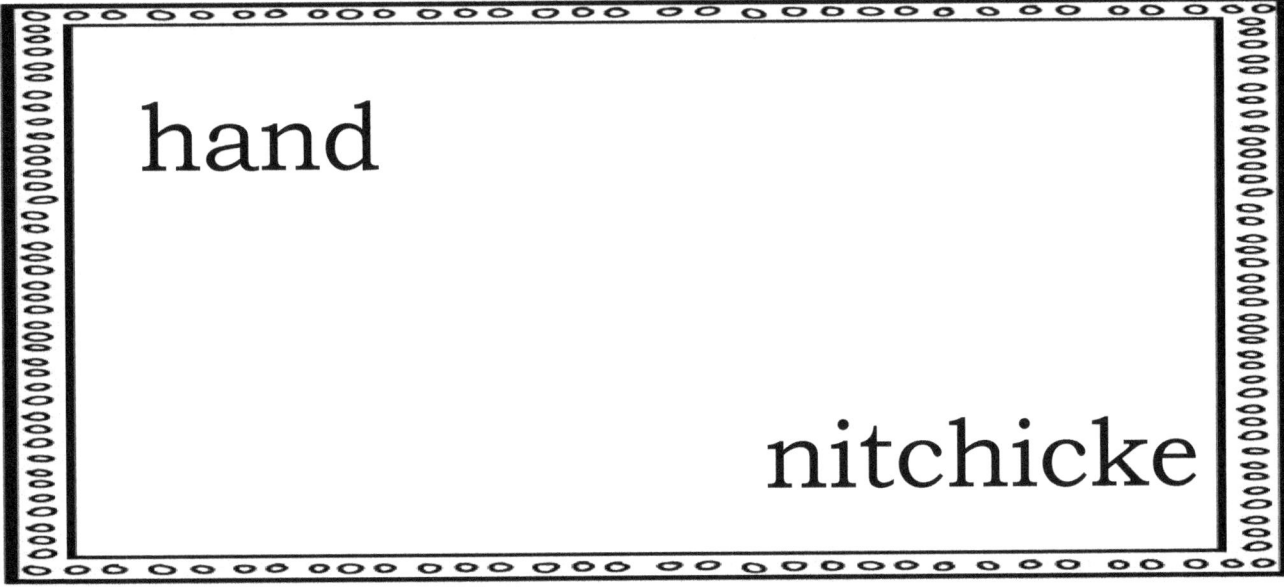

hand

nitchicke

sun

cone

moon

appause

water

nippe

white

wompey

red — squi

house — wetu

mother — nitka

father	noesho
bone	muskana
head	boquoquo

Name: _____ Date: _____

#3 Wampanoag Folklore

Story telling and mythological figures were part of the Wampanoag culture. Read about some of the important Wampanoag mythological figures below, choose one and write your own myth with the character you selected as your protagonist.

Kehtannit: Kehtannit is the great spirit. Kehtannit is the Wampanoag name for the Creator. Kehtannit is the divine spirit with no human form and is never personified, or made to be a person, in Wampanoag folklore or legend. Pronunciation: Kay-tan-nit

Moshup: Moshup is the giant or transformer. He is associated with whales – in most traditions he catches whales to feed the people. Moshup has a wife named Squannit, who is a powerful medicine woman who specializes in children. Pronunciation: Moh-shup or maw-shup

Nikommo: Nikommo are "benevolent little people of the forest", perhaps like fairies. They bring good fortune and help to people who are kind to them.

Pukwudgie: They are magical little people as well. But they are dangerous, more like goblins. They harass people – both innocently and seriously as the situation calls for.

Hobbomock: Hobbomock is the spirit of death. It is viewed as evil.

Horned Serpent: Horned serpents are huge, scaly, dragon-like beings with horns and long teeth. Sometimes they move about on the land, but are more often found in lakes and rivers. Horned serpents are usually very supernatural. They possess magical powers like shape-shifting, invisibility, or hypnotic powers; bestowing powerful medicine upon humans who defeat them or help them; controlling storms and weather, and so on-- and were venerated as gods or spirit beings in some tribes.

The Thunder Bird: The Thunder Bird is described as a huge eagle. It is large enough to carry off a child.

Instructions: Write and illustrate an eight panel story.

Name: _____ Date: _____

Rough Draft Title:

My Story Elements – My Own Wampanoag Tale	
Main Character:	
Character Traits:	
Supporting Character:	
Character Traits:	
Setting:	
Problem:	
Solution:	
Moral:	
Magic:	

Name: _____ Date: _____

#4 Rough Draft Title:

_____

Name: _____ Date: _____

Rough Draft Title Page 2

_____

_____

_____

_____

_____

_____

_____

_____

_____

_____

_____

_____

_____

_____

_____

_____

_____
_____

_____
_____
_____

Name: _____ Date: _____

4 My Notebook Wampanoag Words

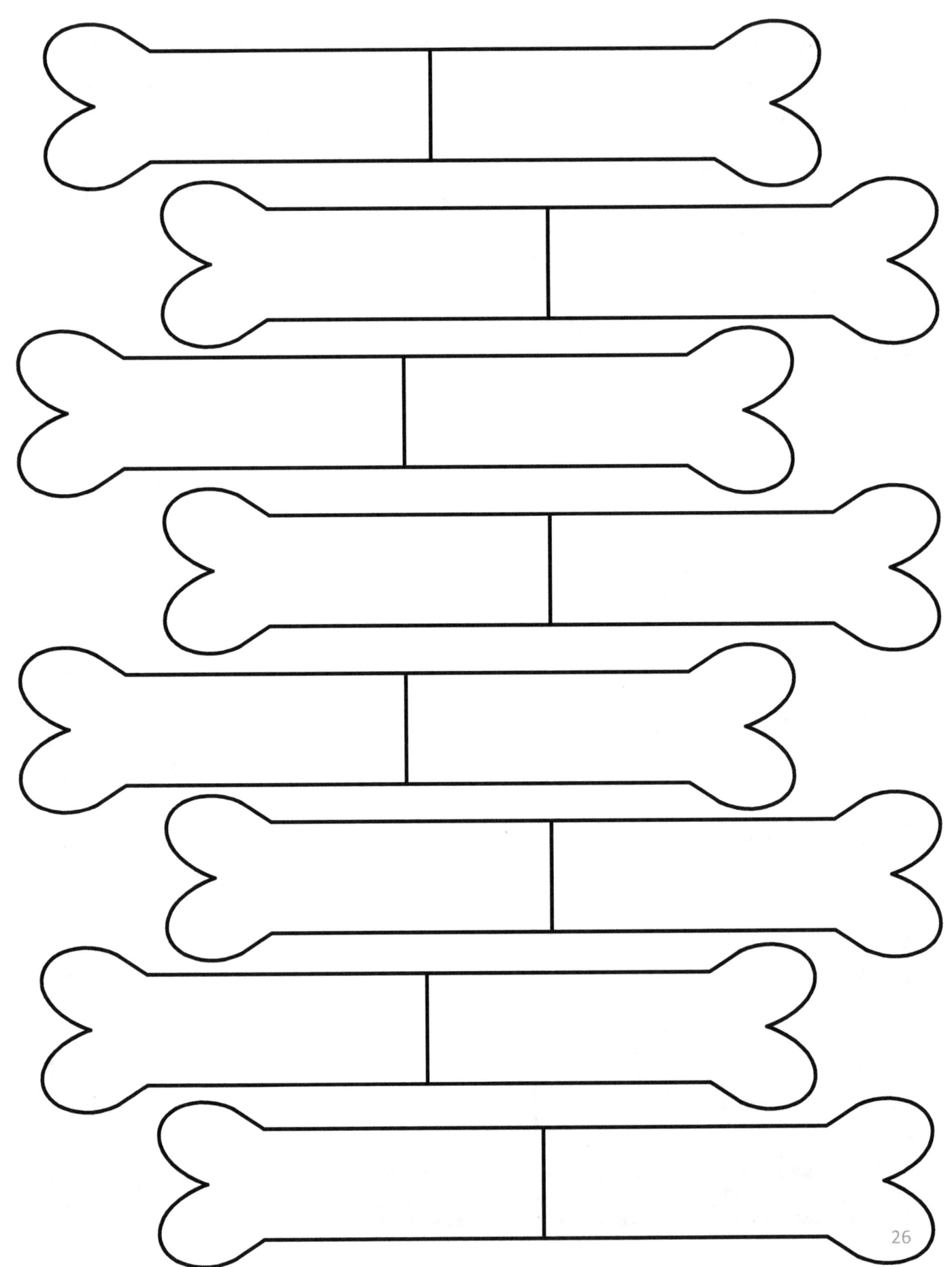

Name: _____ Date: _____

#5 Before The First Thanksgiving

By the time the Pilgrims arrived at Plymouth Rock, a deadly epidemic, caused by a shipwreck, nearly killed off all of the Wampanoag. This was the Great Epidemic of 1616-1619. The ship that wrecked was a French trading ship.

In 1600 the Wampanoag probably numbered around 12,000. There were also about 40 villages. The villages were on the mainland and the off-shore islands of Martha's Vineyard and Nantucket.

The epidemics whipped out at least 10 villages.

When the pilgrims arrived, the surviving Wampanoag were afraid of the Europeans. They believed that the God of these foreigners had sent the epidemic to wipe them out. This fear was further fueled when nearly half of the Pilgrims died during the first winter spent in Plymouth.

The Wampanoag were not fond of the Europeans. The tolerated them and did not attack them because they feared the wrath of the European God.

A visitor to Plymouth in 1621, a man named Robert Cushman, said that the Great Epidemic changed the Native Americans. "[T]heir countenance is dejected," he wrote, "and they seem as a people affrighted" even though they "might in one hour have made a dispatch of us, yet such a fear was upon them, … that they never offered us the least injury in word or deed."

Think and Write:

What happened to the Native Americans? _____
_____
_____
_____
_____
_____

How did the "Great Epidemic" change the Native Americans? _____
_____
_____
_____
_____
_____

Cook, "The Significance of Disease in the Extinction of the New England Indians," *Human Biology* (1973) 45: 485–508.
John S. Marr and John T. Cathey, "New Hypothesis for Cause of Epidemic among Native Americans, New England, 1616–1619" *Emerging Infectious Disease* (Feb 2000) http://wwwnc.cdc.gov/eid/article/16/2/09-0276.htm
William Cronon, *Changes in the Land: Indians, Colonists and the Ecology of New England* (New York: Hill & Wang; 1983).

Name: _____ Date: _____

#6 The First Thanksgiving – It Was Really Lincoln
Primary Source Document Analysis

Every year, on the fourth Thursday in November, people in the United States celebrate Thanksgiving. Did you know that this was not always the case? It was Abraham Lincoln, during the Civil War, who started it all. President Lincoln was upset because the war was dividing families and he wanted all families in the United States to sit down to a meal and give thanks.

On October 20, 1864, President Abraham Lincoln passed Proclamation 118. The proclamation is below. It is a bit difficult to read. Pair or group up, read it and as a group write what it says using your own words.

By the President of the United States of America
A Proclamation

It has pleased Almighty God to prolong our national life another year, defending us with His guardian care against unfriendly designs from abroad and vouchsafing to us in His mercy many and signal victories over the enemy, who is of our own household. It has also pleased our Heavenly Father to favor as well our citizens in their homes as our soldiers in their camps and our sailors on the rivers and seas with unusual health. He has largely augmented our free population by emancipation and by immigration, while He has opened to us new sources of wealth and has crowned the labor of our workingmen in every department of industry with abundant rewards. Moreover, He has been pleased to animate and inspire our minds and hearts with fortitude, courage, and resolution sufficient for the great trial of civil war into which we have been brought by our adherence as a nation to the cause of freedom and humanity, and to afford to us reasonable hopes of an ultimate and happy deliverance from all our dangers and afflictions:

Now, therefore, I, Abraham Lincoln, President of the United States, do hereby appoint and set apart the last Thursday in November next as a day which I desire to be observed by all my fellow-citizens, wherever they may then be, as a day of thanksgiving and praise to Almighty God, the beneficent Creator and Ruler of the Universe. And I do further recommend to my fellow-citizens aforesaid that on that occasion they do reverently humble themselves in the dust and from thence offer up penitent and fervent prayers and supplications to the Great Disposer of Events for a return of the inestimable blessings of peace, union, and harmony throughout the land which it has pleased Him to assign as a dwelling place for ourselves and for our posterity throughout all generations.

In testimony whereof I have hereunto set my hand and caused the seal of the United States to be affixed.

Done at the city of Washington, this 20th day of October, A.D. 1864, and of the Independence of the United States the eighty-ninth.

ABRAHAM LINCOLN.
By the President:
WILLIAM H. SEWARD,
Secretary of State .

Name: _____ Date: _____

#7 The Mayflower

How would you like to leave your home, with 100 other people and some farm animals – for 66 days and travel on a small ship to a place you've never been? That's what the Pilgrims did in the year 1620, on a ship called Mayflower.

Public Domain Image

The Mayflower

Mayflower set sail from England in July 1620, but it had to turn back twice because Speedwell, the ship it was traveling with, leaked. After deciding to leave the leaky Speedwell behind, Mayflower finally got underway on September 6, 1620.

In the 1600s, the ocean was a dangerous place. Ships could be attacked and taken over by pirates. Ships were also often shipwrecked by storms.
Passengers sometimes fell overboard and drowned or got sick and died too.

We know that the Mayflower did not sink, but a few of these dangerous things actually did happen! First, the ship was damaged by a bad storm halfway to America. The storm cracked one of the wooden beams that supported the ships mainframe. The passengers had to fix it in the middle of the ocean. Another storm swept a young man off the deck of the ship and into the ocean! He was saved because he grabbed onto one of the ship's ropes and was pulled back onto the deck. One person died on the voyage and a baby was born.

It was a rough ride with a lot of seasick people. The picture at the top of the page is a public domain image of the ship. It looks big, but not according to today's standards.

Think and Write

Imagine you are a passenger aboard the Mayflower and you have just arrived on the shores of the New World. Write a letter home about your journey.

Name: _____ Date: _____

#8 The Landing

After about two months at sea – two months! Sixty-six days to be exact, the Pilgrims finally landed at Cape Cod. They date was November 11, 1620. A few weeks later, they sailed up the coast to Plymouth and began to build their town where a group of Wampanoag people had lived . The village was now deserted because of the Great Epidemic that hit the Native Americans so hard .

The Pilgrims lived on the ship for a few more months, rowing ashore to build houses during the day, but going back to sleep on the ship at night. Many people began to get sick from the cold and the wet. It was now December and the weather was harsh. About half the people on the *Mayflower* died that first winter from what they described as a "general sickness" of colds, coughs and fevers.

Finally, in March 1621, there were enough houses for everyone to live on land. After a long, hard voyage, and an even harder winter, the *Mayflower* left Plymouth to return to England. The date was April 5, 1621.

Think and Write
Draw a two panel comic illustrating the first winter for the Europeans along the Eastern shores of what is now Massachusetts.

Name: _____   Date: _____

9 The MayFlower Compact

So why'd they really come?

   We know the Mayflower brought the Pilgrims to the New World in 1620. The journey across the Atlantic Ocean was harsh. Passengers traveled in the cargo hold of the ship – where the air was heavy and it smelled horrible. The ship swayed with the waves and the people were often sick. The trip took two months.

   The Pilgrims came to the New World so that they could practice the religion they wanted. They couldn't do that in England. There everyone had to belong to the Church of England.

   The Pilgrims went from England to the Netherlands. They could be any religion they wanted there, but they didn't want to be Dutch. So, they set out to build their own society.

   The Virginia Company agreed to pay the way for the Pilgrims to come to the New World. The Pilgrims had to agree to repay The Virginia Company with lumber and furs from their new home.

   The Pilgrims were also called Separatists because they wanted to build their own religion and their own society.

   The Pilgrims were not headed to Plymouth Rock where they landed. They were off course, but there were great things about landing in Cape Cod – where Plymouth Rock is. For one thing, it had a harbor. Plus, it had fresh water nearby. They had good farmland. The bad thing was that it was far away from Virginia, so they had no government or laws to protect them.

   To keep order, all of the men on board the Mayflower signed a contract called the Mayflower Compact. They all agreed on fair laws made for the good of the colony. They agreed they would govern themselves. This meant that everyone who signed the Mayflower
Compact had a right to help make the laws they would live by. This was a system of majority rules. This is a democratic idea and one of the most important parts of our government today. Even the people who crossed the Atlantic realized the importance of majority rules.

Think and Write

Write a paragraph about what you think would be the most important laws for the new land and why.

_____
_____
_____
_____
_____

10 Plymouth Colony What Would You Do?

Name: _____   Date: _____

The Plymouth Colony – What Would You Do…

Imagine you are the Captain of a ship sailing to the New World in 1620. You land on a beautiful rocky beach. You feel happy to be alive and to have all of the people you brought with you alive as well.

But, you traveled through some horrible storms. These storms threw you off course. You have to start a new settlement. What would you do? What do you think the most important thing to do would be? What types of things would you need to survive?

Make a list of the first things you'd have to do when you arrived. You are the Captain and everyone is looking to you to keep them safe. Rank your list in order of importance.

_____
_____
_____
_____
_____
_____
_____
_____
_____
_____

Name: _____ Date: _____

11 My Compact

The Mayflower Compact or The _____ Compact

You've completed your list and you realize that you have no laws and no government. You gather all of the people together and decide to make a compact, or set, of laws for the good of the community.

Name your compact and then write it out below. Be sure to use complete sentences.

_____
_____
_____
_____
_____
_____
_____
_____
_____
_____
_____
_____
_____
_____
_____
_____
_____
_____
_____
_____

Name: _____ Date: _____

#12 The Pilgrims

Recap: The people who made up the Plymouth Colony were a group of English Protestants who wanted to break away from the Church of England. They were called 'separatists'. First they moved to Holland, but it did not go well there. After about 12 years of financial problems, they received funding from English merchants to sail across the Atlantic to settle in a 'New World.'

They intended to sail to New York, but the windy conditions brought them to Plymouth Rock.

Pilgrim Facts:
- Their clothes were not all black
- The Pilgrims did not land on an unknown frontier. The waters off New England were fished by the English for at least 100 years before the they landed and lived on for nearly 15,000 years by Native Americans
- The Pilgrims used the word "corn" to describe wheat, rye, barley, oats, peas, and beans. They used the term "Indian corn" or "turkey wheat" when speaking of what we now call corn.
- In the Pilgrim household, the adults sat down to dinner and the children waited on them.

Think and Write

Compare and contrast .

Pilgrims from Stories

Similarities

What I just read about Pilgrims

Achiq
The Wampanoag Cinderella

Common Core State Standards Aligned

Companion Unit for
Achiq: The Wampanoag Cinderella
By Elizabeth Chapin-Pinotti

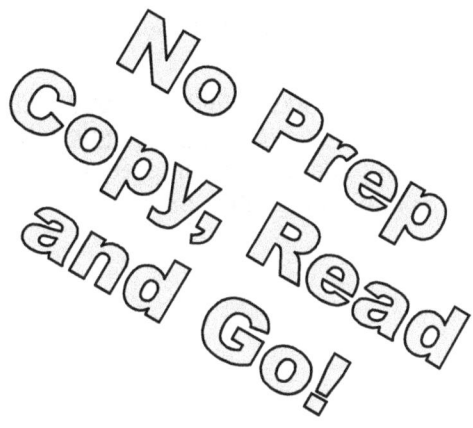

No Prep
Copy, Read
and Go!

Table of Contents

The Story
Cinderella Elements
#1: <u>Achiq The Wampanoag Cinderella</u> Problem Solution Interactive Notebook Page
#2: <u>Achiq The Wampanoag Cinderella</u> Character Traits RL.3
#3: Character Traits RL.3
#4: Critical Thinking Literature Questions Interactive Notebook Page
#5: Ask and Answer Questions on Illustrations RL.7
#6: Inferring RL.6
#7: <u>Achiq The Wampanoag Cinderella</u> – What do you think? RL.1 and 3
#8: Problem/Solution Interactive Notebook Page RL.5
#9: Critical Thinking Questions
#10: About <u>Achiq The Wampanoag Cinderella</u> RL 1 and 2
#11: Recounting <u>Achiq The Wampanoag Cinderella</u>
#12: Character Motivation and Evidence RL.5
#13: Visualize the Future
#14 <u>Achiq The Wampanoag Cinderella</u>: Character Conflicts RL.1 and 3
#15 Sentence Sorting RL.2   Answers: 5,4,2,6,7,3,1
#16 From Sentence Sorting to Essay Writing RL1 and 2
#17: Quick Write: Compare and Contrast RL.9
#18: Text-to-Text RL.9
#19: I Can Answer Questions About the Text RL.1
#20: Notes to Author: Critical Thinking Activity
#21: Moral RL.2
#22: Inferring RL.6
#23 Retell the Story through your Favorite Drawings RL.7
#24: Cause and Effect
#25: <u>The Achiq The Wampanoag Cinderella</u> Report Card
#26: <u>The Achiq The Wampanoag Cinderella</u> Book Review
#27: Quiz Multiple Choice Comprehension– The Wampanoag a, d, d, a, c, d
Rubric for Constructed Response

Achiq – The Wampanoag Cinderella

Long before the Mayflower dropped anchor off the shores of Plymouth Rock, a proud and noble people worked the land and the ocean and called what would one day be known as Massachusetts home. The Wampanoag, or People of the First Light, lived on their land for over fifteen thousand years before travelers from other regions of the world knew this land existed. Their homeland was bountiful and life was good.

The Great Spirit, Kehtannit, bestowed many gifts upon the hardworking people as they foraged the forests and valleys in the hard cold winters and basked in the sunshine of the rivers and ponds and the wide wild ocean when the weather warmed. For centuries crops were abundant and fish and game abounded.

Along about 1616, a French merchant ship wreaked off the shores of Cape Cod. The survivors brought with them small pox and other diseases that devastated the Wampanoag people— very few survived.

Before the plagues, Achiq had a happy childhood, frolicking in the forests in the winter and sowing crops of squash, beans and maize in the summer, but her favorite pastime was helping her many aunts and mother dig for clams on the windy shores of the Atlantic Ocean. Only when disease took her mother and loving aunts, and Achiq was left alone with her father, Achak, did she feel loneliness.

Achiq took solace in the running rivers and hid her tears in the whipping wind of the bitter Northeastern winter. She kept busy with her crops and clams until winter came again and then she started the task her mother had only just begun teaching her – the making of the family clothes.

In the time of sixteen moons, her father remarried and he and Achiq welcomed Chepi and her daughters into their wetu. Achak was a great warrior and diplomat and often worked away from home with his brother, the great chief Massasoit.

Chepi was a kind woman, but her daughters were not. Chepi worked hard alongside Achiq, helping the young warrior princess learn to work the soft deer skin into breechcloth while her own two blood daughters ran about the village and took to spying on the white people who had come to settle on the shores where once a sister Algonquin village stood.

As the sun began to rise and set high in the sky, it was announced that the great harvest feast would be hosted in a neighboring village to give thanks for the abundant beans and maize crops gifted to the land by the Great Spirit that autumn.

Achiq's breath caught in her throat when it was proclaimed that the son of a neighboring chief was ready for a bride and that one would be selected at the celebration. The young warrior was Annawan and he was glorious. All of the squaws, from the farthest north to the deepest south knew of Annawan, his bravery against the foreigners and his beauty, inside and out. Groups of young girls gathered for a glimpse of him and mothers fussed over their daughters in hopes of one day winning his hand – whenever he graced their villages with his presence.

Achiq admired the young brave. She too thought he was breathless – and although she was young among the other squaws – her father was well respected – her uncle was the chief of their village and she secretly hoped the young man would fall in love with her.

"Nitka, Mother," Achiq said softly by the glow of the fire one evening while she was helping her stepmother prepare the evening meal. "Will you help me sew a dress so beautiful that Annawan will at least know I am alive?"

Her stepmother smiled at her modesty. Achiq was a beautiful girl, the image of her birth mother, with a heart as pure as the river that raged through the forest and eyes as deep as the moonless sky. "Of course my child. You will have the most spectacular dress the world has ever seen and you will wear my best jewelry, made from the finest shells in the ocean."

Achiq's two stepsisters were lurking in the darkness nearby and heard the exchange.

"How could mother betray us!" one scoffed.

"She will not get away with it. That child will not win the heart of Annawan. He is mine! I am oldest, dear sister, and should marry first. We, of course, will care for you,' said the second. "Come, I've an idea."

The morning of the festival was harried for everyone. Food was prepared, clothes were readied and all were buzzing with thoughts of singing and dancing and feasting.

Chepi and Achak were part of the grand ceremony and left their village early – leaving the girls alone to get ready.

"We will be fine parents," the oldest stepdaughter said. "I will make sure my sisters are dressed and get safely to the festival."

Before leaving, Chepi handed Achiq a small pouch. In it was a necklace of the deepest blue the girl had ever seen. The color matched the shells on the warrior princess' new dress.

"Let your inner radiance shine brighter than the shells, child, that is the way to Annawan's heart."

The parents left and Achiq busied herself attaching the last shells to her dress. As she held it out to admire the garment a loud explosion shook the ground. Achiq dropped the dress and turned to see the family wetu ablaze!

She quickly grabbed a basket and raced for the creek than ran into the ocean. The oldest sister snatched the dress and the necklace and the two hurried off to the festival, leaving Achiq to fit with the fire alone.

The village empty because of the festivities, Achiq ran back and forth with the basket, finally putting out the flames. The outer portion of their home was singed and a large hole let in the light of the day, but the warrior princess acted quickly and prevented too much damage.

Exhausted, Achiq sat on a rock and surveyed the ground for her dress and the pouch containing her stepmothers jewels, but they were gone. She looked down at the dress she wore, black with the soot and ashes from the fire and sighed. It was a wreck. A tear rolled down her cheek. She had nothing clean and spectacular to wear, she was covered in cinders and she was exhausted.

As she was wondering what to do a great wind whisked over the charred wetu. It swept up from the sea as a tiny Nikommo appeared from the forest beyond the beach.

"Hello," Achiq said a bit startled. She'd heard of the tiny fairies but had never seen one.

"I am Strava," the Nikommo said, "I am here at the calling of the Great Spirit." The tiny creature spun in a circle, pulling the wind with her. When the wind subsided, Achiq was adorned in the most enchanting clothing she had ever seen and her jewelry sparkled as it caught the sun that was now setting in the sky.

"Oh thank you kind little Nikommo," the girl said, "but I will never make it to the feast on time."

The ground began to quake again. From out of the sea rose Moshup riding on the back of an enormous whale. "Come," the benevolent giant beckoned to Achiq, "we will ride to the festival together."

Strava twirled again and the wind carried Achiq onto the back of the whale and together she and Moshup sailed along the shoreline.

They arrived as the festival was about to begin – from sundown to sun up all would celebrate the harvest. The crowd hushed as the great giant placed Achiq in the center of the celebration. Her stepmother looked up at her and beyond her – where her oldest blood daughter sat – next to Annawan in the dress made for Achiq in the jewels loaned to Achiq.

Chepi's eyes grew narrow and her heart filled with rage and she headed to her oldest daughter, only her husband stopped her.

"The battle is not yours. It is cast to the Great Spirit. Let the pure heart prevail," he said calmly.

"That is not the way it works, husband," she said. "That is not the way of the world. A wrong must be righted."

Just then Annawan's eyes caught the tiny warrior princess'. She smiled shyly and he rose.

The stepsister grabbed his arm, but he barely noticed as he made his way to the most beautiful girl he had ever seen. A gentle wind brushed his back as he walked to her.

They eat and danced and spoke well into the morning and in the time of five moons they were married and set on a course that would chart the history of their villages as well as the greater world around them.

As they shared their early love, neither knew of the changes on the winds of time destined to alter their very existence.

Cinderella Elements

Teacher Note: Please be sensitive to students who may be members of blended families. The stereotypes of "stepmothers" and "stepsisters" that are part of many Cinderella stories must be carefully addressed.

Check out my other Cinderella Units at https://www.teacherspayteachers.com/Store/Elizabeths-Lessons. Before you explore any of the versions, including this one, it is imperative to discuss the basic aspects of Cinderella in general with your students. The best way to do so is by using elements of active participation.

For discussion: Cinderella stories are considered folk tales or fairy tales. Folk tales and fairy tales are legends or stories handed down from generation to generation – usually orally. These stories are considered folk tales until they are written down…once they are on paper…they are considered fairy tales. Folk tales and fairy tales have common themes that transcend many cultures and often contain life lessons, global truths and/or explain things that happen in nature. Most folk tales and fairy include the following elements:

A beginning – or a "Once upon a time…"
Magic of some sort
Royalty or a social hierarchy
A wicked character
A kind and or thoughtful character who is usually treated badly
Goodness rewarded in the end

Explore the above elements with students. It is helpful to put up a Cinderella from around the world bulletin board with sections for each element. After you finish with each story…put the Cinderella story name on the board and brainstorm the elements… listing them next to the story. If this is done in grid form…students will easily be able to compare stories.

Having a large map and placing colorful pins on the location points of the stories as you read is a great visual for students to link the commonalities of what they are reading to the vastness of the world.

After you discuss the main Cinderella elements, do the Sentence Sorting and From Sentence Sorting to Essay Writing activities from the instruction pages as guided lessons with your students. It will help them learn the templates, reinforce structure and organization of sentences and essays and reinforce the Cinderella elements.

#1

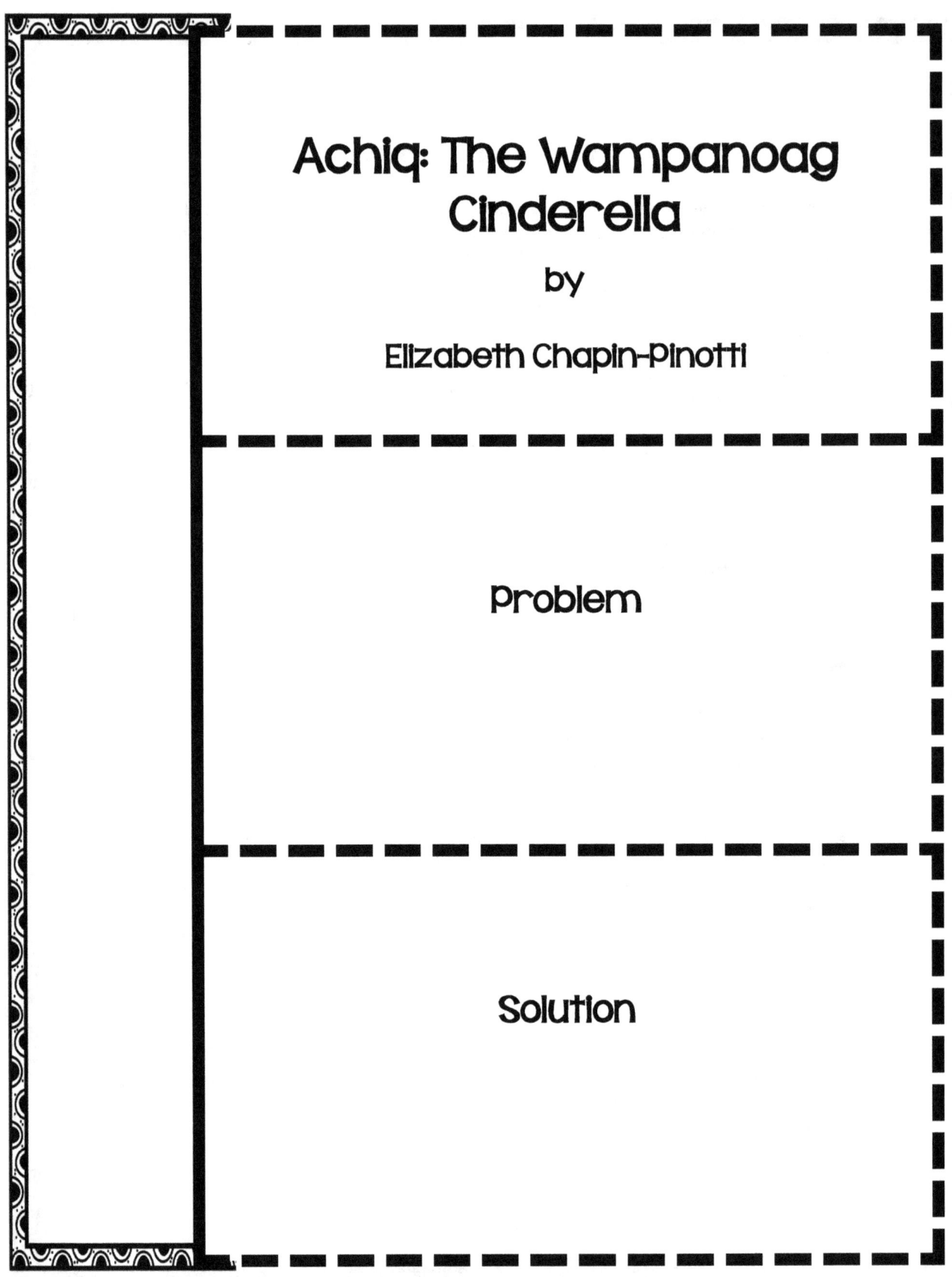

Achiq: The Wampanoag Cinderella

by

Elizabeth Chapin-Pinotti

Problem

Solution

#2

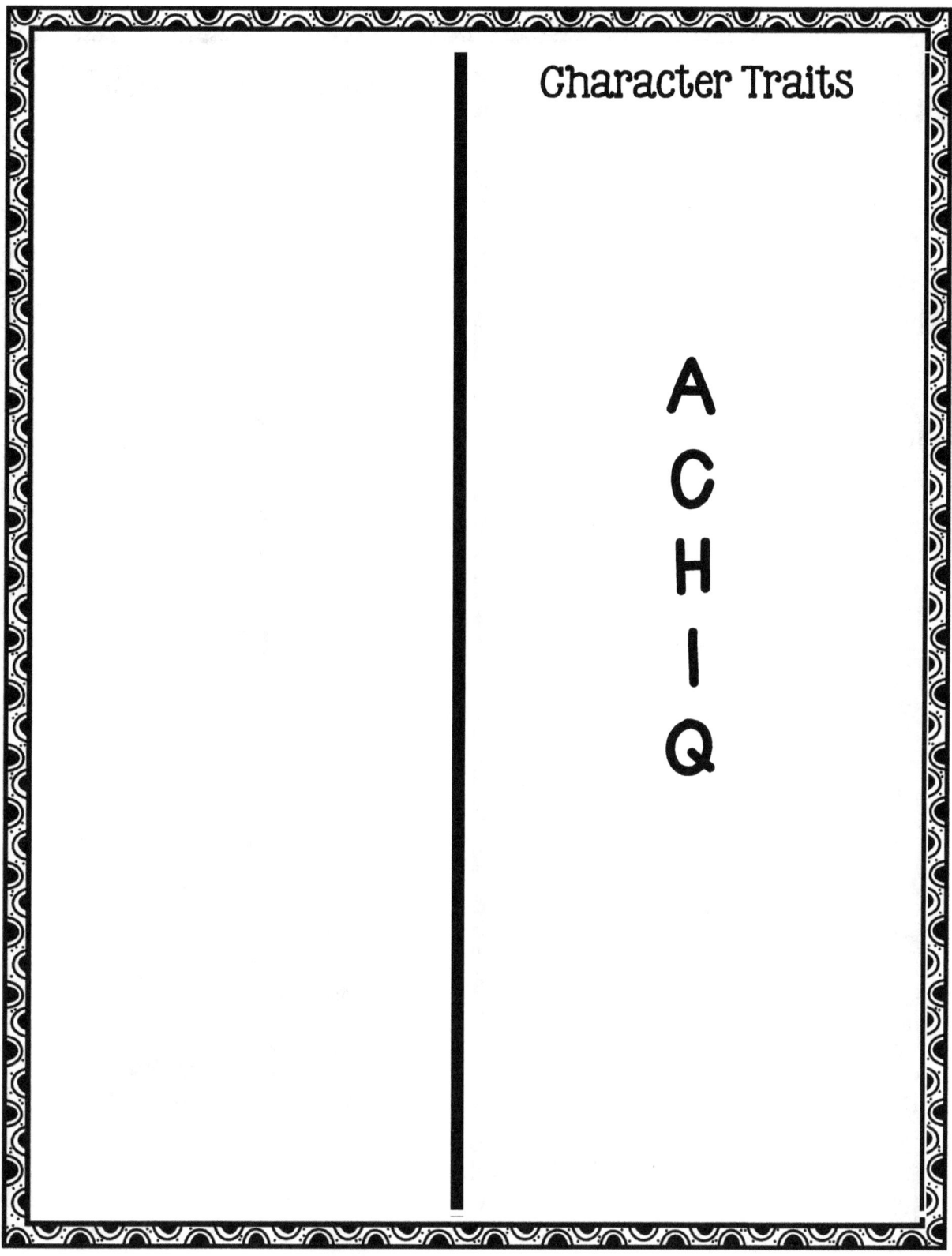

Cut along the outer lines. #3

Cut along the dots.

#4

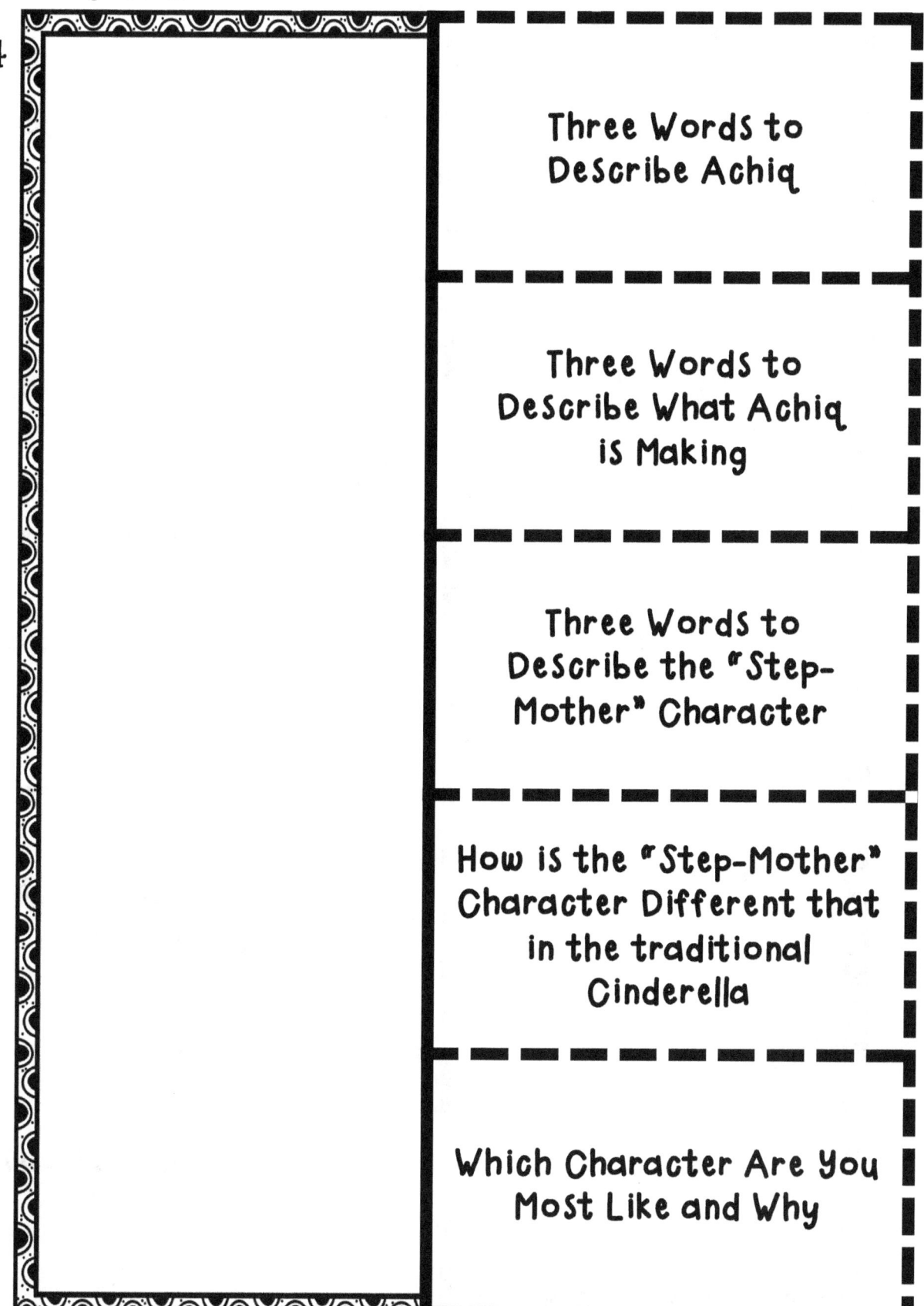

Three Words to Describe Achiq

Three Words to Describe What Achiq is Making

Three Words to Describe the "Step-Mother" Character

How is the "Step-Mother" Character Different that in the traditional Cinderella

Which Character Are You Most Like and Why

#5 Cut along the dots.

What stands out for you in the illustrations?

What does that tell you about mood?

What does it tell about setting?

What does it tell about character(s)?

How do the illustrations make you feel?

Determining Importance
I can read and understand grade level text!

RL 10
#6

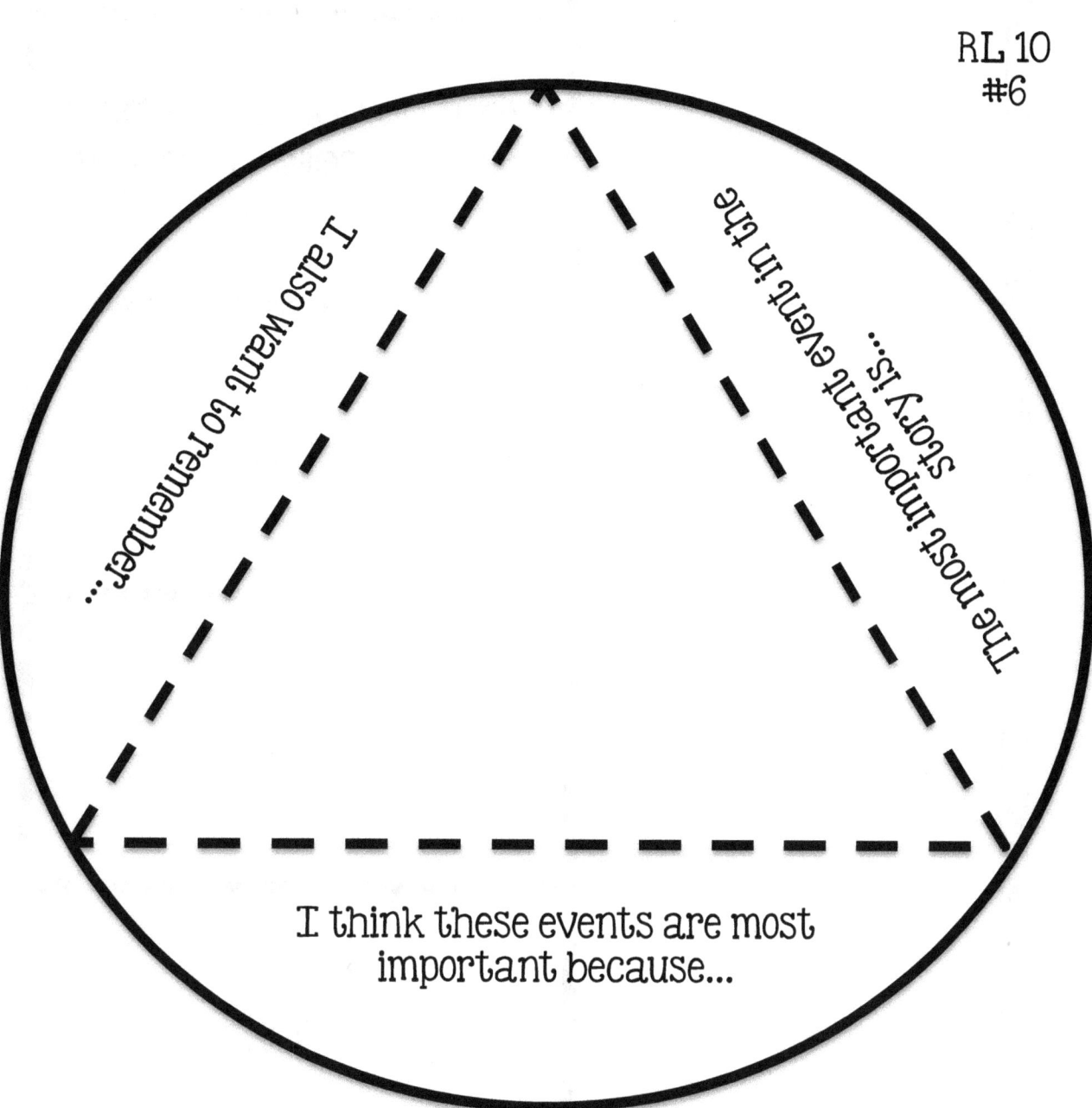

The most important event in the story is...

I also want to remember...

I think these events are most important because...

Cut along the bubbles.

#7

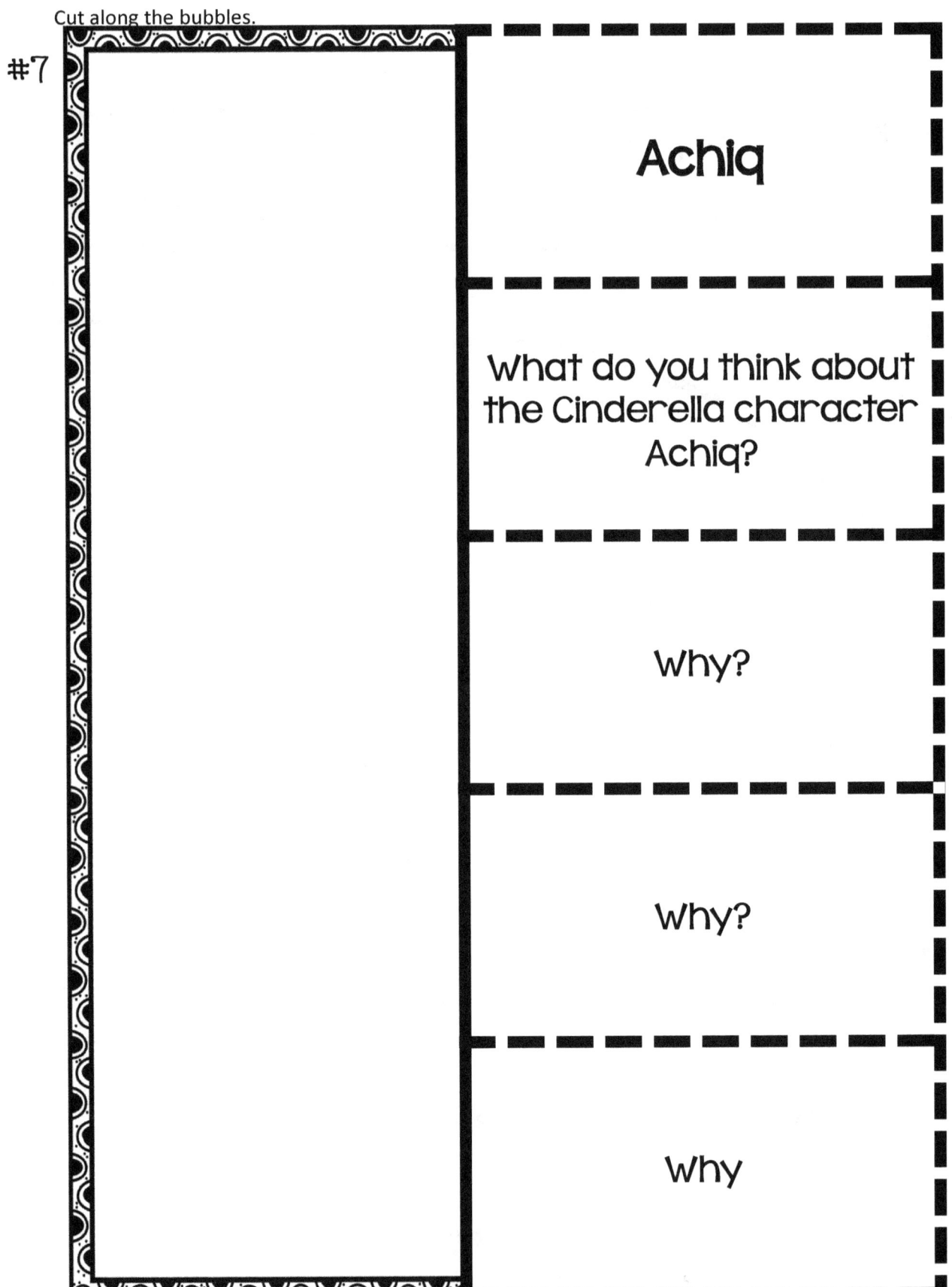

Achiq

What do you think about the Cinderella character Achiq?

Why?

Why?

Why

#9

What is different about Achiq than many of the other Cinderella characters?

_____

How is Achiq different from her step-sisters?

Describe what you think the harvest festival would be like.

Cut along the dotted line. Paste along the solid line. Write under the flap.

About Achiq The Wampanoag Cinderella #10

What is your favorite part of the story? _____
_____

Details why…
1. _____
_____

2. _____
_____

Who is your favorite character? _____
_____

Details why…
1. _____
_____

2. _____
_____

What is the main problem or conflict in the story? _____
_____

Details…
1. _____
_____

2. _____
_____

Summarize Achig The Wampanoag Cinderella

In the beginning…

After that…

Later…

Just when…

At the end…

Cut along dashed line. RL 2 #11

Glue this to your notebook.

In the beginning _____
_____
_____
_____

After that _____
_____
_____
_____
_____
_____

Later _____
_____
_____
_____
_____
_____

Just when _____
_____
_____
_____
_____

At the end _____
_____
_____
_____
_____

Motivation and Evidence

What is Achiq's Motivation
Plus...
Evidence to Support My Thoughts

What is Step-Sister One's Motivation
Plus...
Evidence to Support My Thoughts

What is the Annawan's Motivation
Plus...
Evidence to Support My Thoughts

Cut along dashed line. #12

Visualize the Future -- #13

Use context clues from the story to draw the following. When you are finished, turn to an elbow partner and discuss why you made the choices you did? What helped you decide what the different houses would look like?

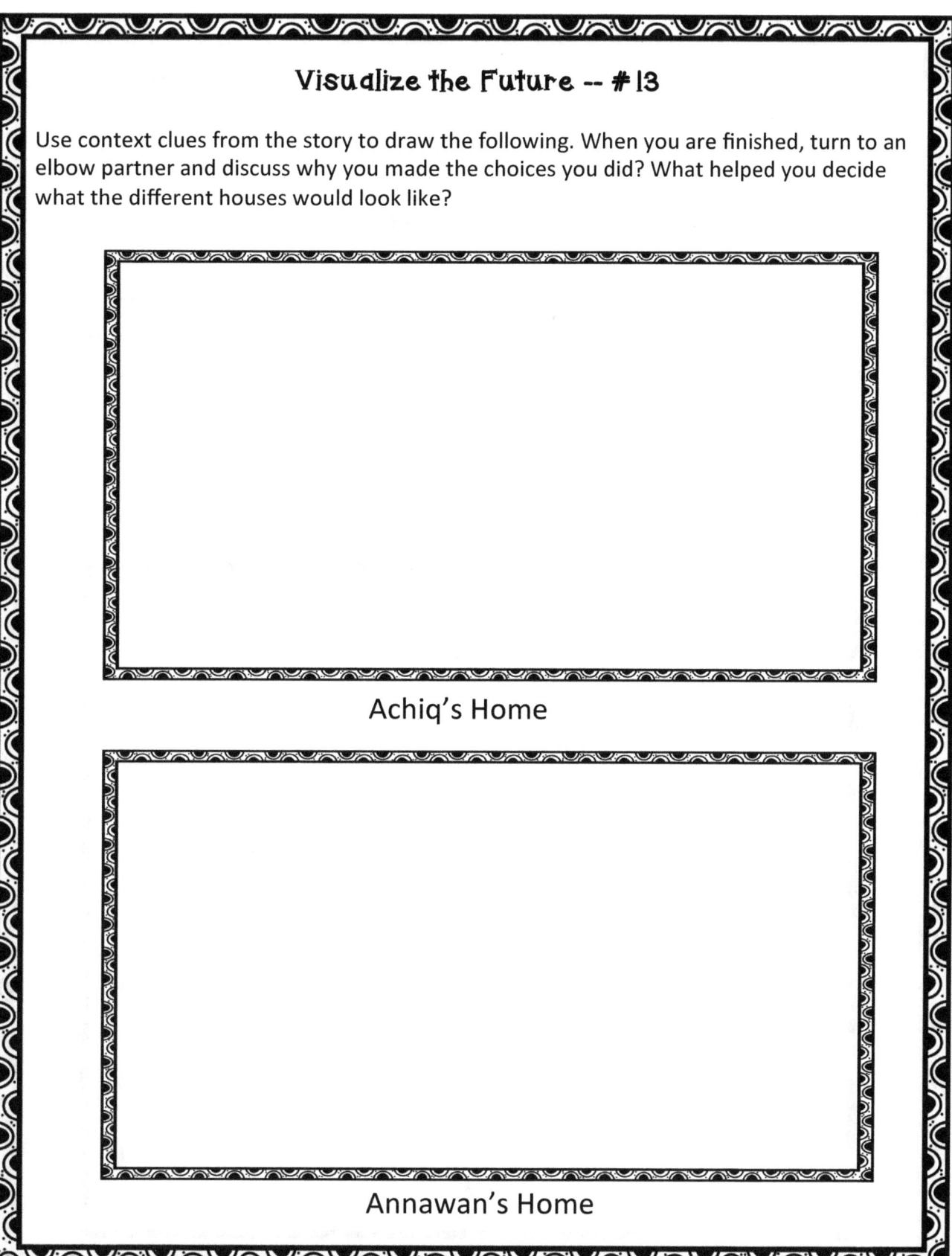

Achiq's Home

Annawan's Home

Achiq The Wampanoag Cinderella Character Conflicts - #14

Character Conflicts: A problem or struggle between two people, things or ideas.

What conflict developed as a result of Grandfather's hunting partner becoming ill?

_____
_____
_____
_____
_____

How would you represent the actions of this conflict using the elements of the graphic novel. Draw it below.

Sentence Sorting – Recounting the Story RL.2 # 15

Cut the sentence strips below and arrange them in the order they appear in the story.

Achiq The Wampanoag Cinderella

1. Achiq and Annawan met and ate, talked and danced all night.

2. Achiq loved to clam with her mother and favorite aunts.

3. Achiq's step-sisters stole Achiq's dress and left her to fight the fire all alone.

4. An epidemic whipped out most of the Wampanoag.

5. The Wampanoag lived on the shores of what is not the Eastern United States for over 15,000 years before Europeans came.

6. Achiq's father married a woman with two daughters.

7. Chepi was kind to Achiq and helped her make a dress for the festival.

Sentence Sorting to Essay Writing Enrichment
Recounting the Story and Making an Argument

From Sentence Sorting to Essay Writing

GOAL: To gain a better understanding of what you read through reading and writing. To have an outline ready to go for an English/Language Arts writing assignment.

Directions:

Copy the template on the next page onto a transparency or use the computer generated sheet on a projector or document camera etc. Copy one blackline master per student.

Do a sample on the board and demonstrate the entire activity to the class – discuss the order of the sentence strips and copy them.

Check for understanding using think, speak and do strategies as you and your students write the essay together.

Review the sentence sorting activity as a group.

Extension Assignment:

- Have students choose a concept idea from the story.
- Have students us the story to write their own sentence strips.
- Re-pair up students with different partners and have them work self-created sentence strips.
- Hand out another template and help students move from sentence strips to essay writing on their own.
- For limited English proficient students and students who need extra help – you may want to do the assignment together – you on the board taking suggestions and them writing it down on their paper. Test and check as you help them to individualize their worksheet as you all move along together.

Hint to Motivate: Copy the template onto paper, laminate and have students use dry erase markers to construct their essays. When the rough draft is complete, have students peer edit and then copy their essays onto notebook paper. This saves time...helps with the editing process and engages students. There is something about dry erase markers and shiny surfaces that students love.

From Sentence Sorting to Essay Writing - #16
Achiq The Wampanoag Cinderella

Paragraph 1: Write down the paragraph you created from your sentence strips.

1.
2.
3.
4.
5.
6.
7.

Paragraph 2: Use one sentence from paragraph 1 as your topic sentence or "Main Idea" for this paragraph and another sentence from paragraph 1 as "Detail 2".

Main Idea:
Detail 1:
Supporting Fact:
Detail 2:
Supporting Fact:
Concluding Sentence:

Paragraph 3: Use one sentence from paragraph 1 as your topic sentence or "Main Idea" for this paragraph and another sentence from paragraph 1 as "Detail 2".

Main Idea:
Detail 1:
Supporting Fact:
Detail 2:
Supporting Fact:
Concluding Sentence:

Paragraph 4: Use one sentence from paragraph 1 as your topic sentence or "Main Idea" for this paragraph and another sentence from paragraph 1 as "Detail 2".

Main Idea:
Detail 1:
Supporting Fact:
Detail 2:
Supporting Fact:
Concluding Sentence:

Paragraph 5 – Conclusion; Use your "Thesis Statement" from paragraph 1 as your **main idea** for this concluding paragraph.

Thesis Statement:
Detail 1:
Supporting Fact:
Detail 2:
Supporting Fact:
Concluding Sentence:

Quick Write Compare and Contrast - #17

Compare the Cinderella from <u>Achiq The Wampanoag Cinderella</u> with the original Cinderella.

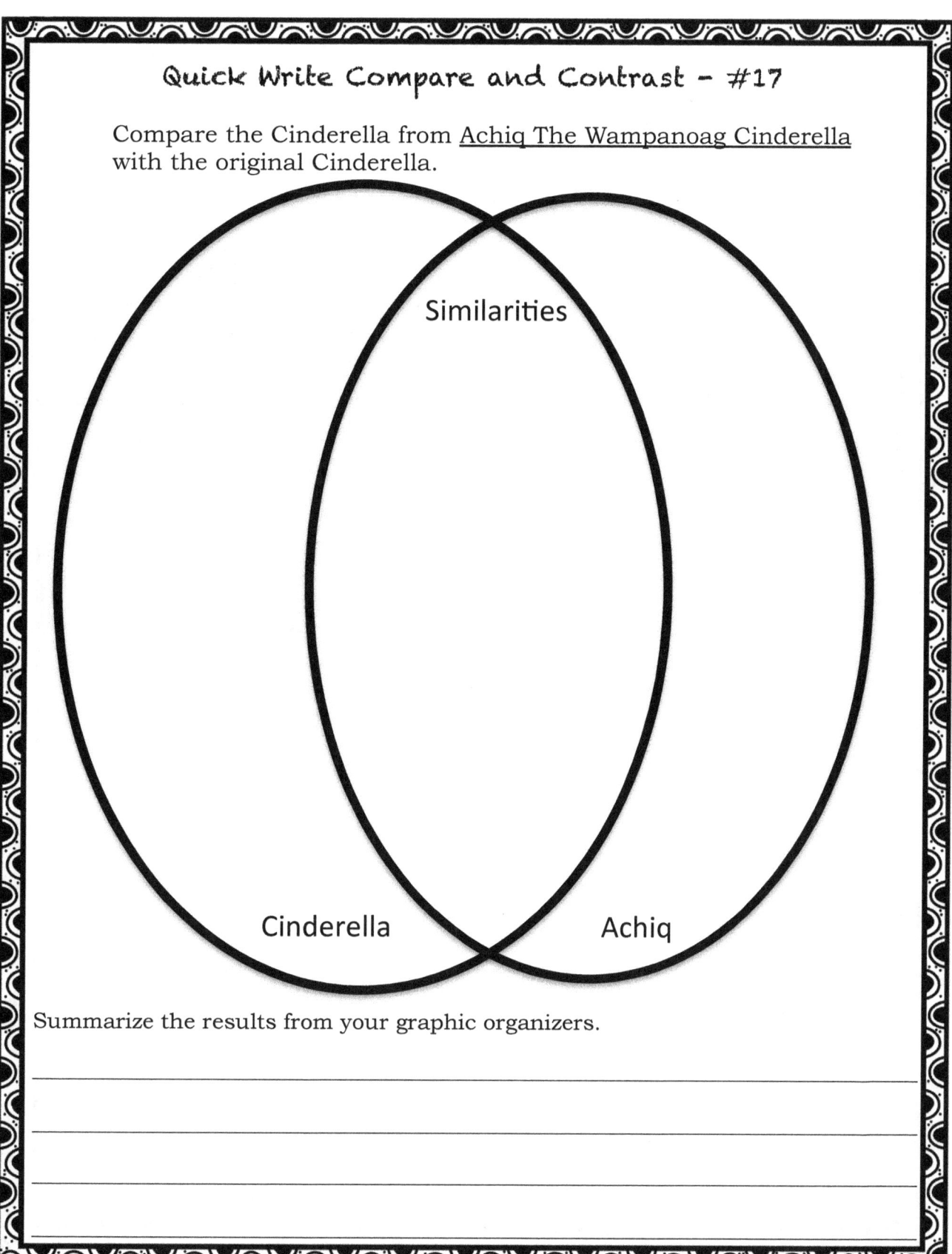

Summarize the results from your graphic organizers.

_____
_____
_____
_____

Text to Text
Connecting Fiction Texts - #18

Achiq The Wampanoag Cinderella

_____
Book Title

How Can You Connect These Two Texts?

I Can Ask and Answer Questions About the Text RL.1
Cut Along the Dashed Lines #19

Question:_____
_____
_____
_____
_____
_____

- -

Question:_____
_____
_____
_____
_____
_____

- -

Question:_____
_____
_____
_____
_____
_____

Answer:_____

_____

_____

_____

_____

_____

Answer:_____

_____

_____

_____

_____

_____

Answer:_____

_____

_____

_____

_____

_____

Notes to the Author #20
A Critical Thinking, Comprehension Activity

What I liked best about the story was _____
_____
_____
_____

One thing I was confused about was _____
_____
_____
_____

One thing I would change is _____
_____
_____
_____

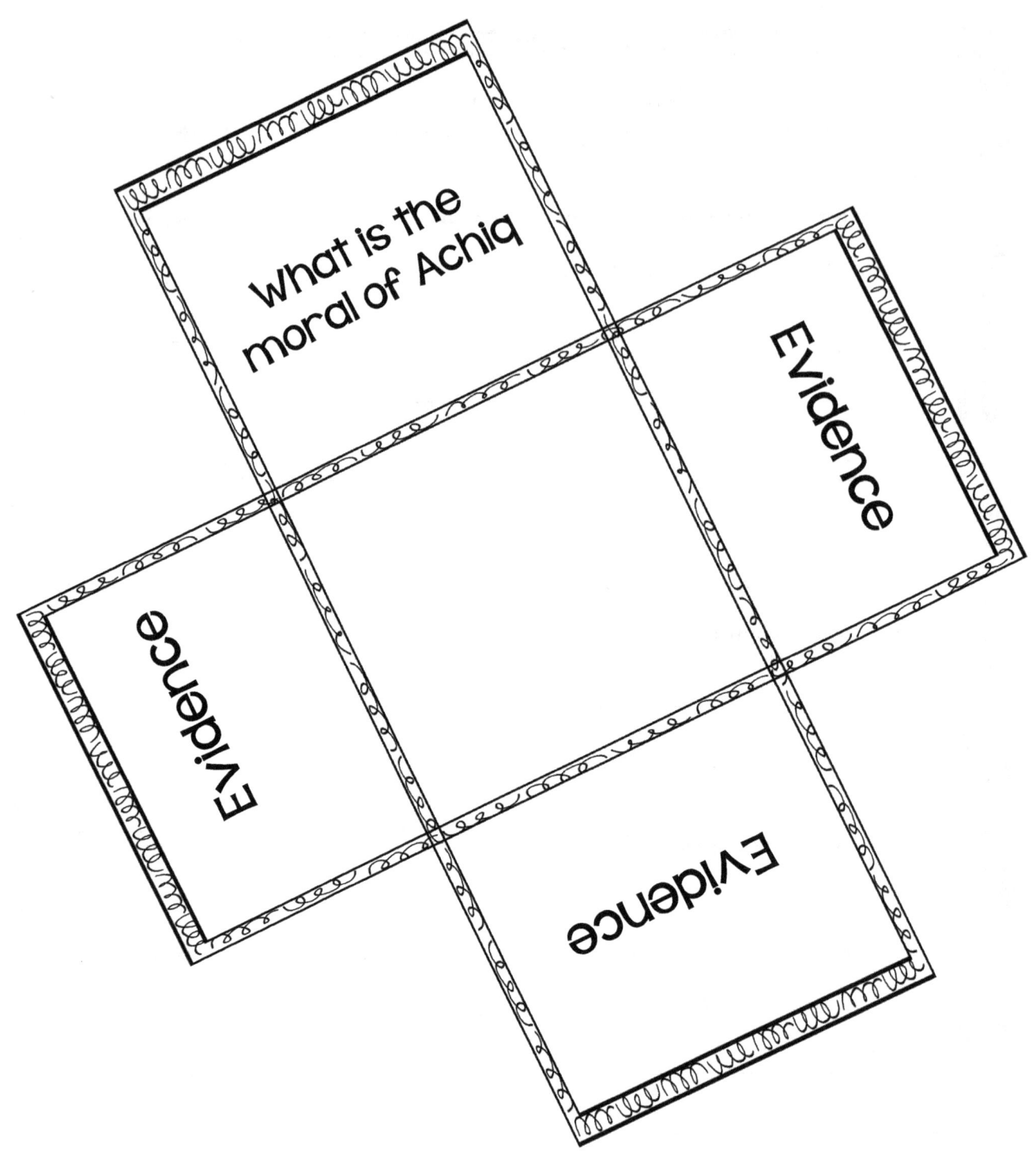

#21 Cut out the foldable, Glue onto your paper. Answer the questions.

#22 Inferring Character
Cut both rectangles…

Glue on top

Achiq The Wampanoag Cinderella

How does she feel: _____
_____
_____
_____
_____
_____
_____
_____

Evidence from Text to Support MY Thinking:
_____
_____
_____
_____
_____
_____

Glue on bottom.

#23: Retell the Story in Drawing
Redraw your favorite pictures from the story.

First,	Then...

Achiq The Wampanoag Cinderella

After that...	Finally,

Name: _____

Cause and Effect- #24

Think about and discuss the cause and effect of Chepi's kindness.

Cause – Because of this……_____
_____
_____
_____
_____
_____

Effect – This happened……_____
_____
_____
_____
_____
_____

Name: _____

Achiq The Wampanoag Cinderella Card #25

Grade	Comments
Setting	
Main Character	
Supporting Characters	
Plot	
Magic	
Beginning	
Conflict	
Ending	

Achiq The Wampanoag Cinderella
Book Review #26

Things I liked about this book: _____
_____
_____
_____

Things I would change about this book: _____
_____
_____
_____

Would you recommend this book and why or why not:_____
_____
_____
_____
_____

Star rating...

☆☆☆☆☆

Signed: _____

The Wampanoag Cinderella Quick Quiz # 27

A great epidemic nearly whipped out the Wampanoag. According to the story, the epidemic was caused by:
   a) Diseases, such as small pox, that resulted from sick people from a shipwrecked boat
   b) French traded who purposely brought disease to the Wampanoag
   c) Poor health care
   d) Annawan's father was sick during the harvest festival and infected everyone else

Before her mother died, Achiq used to:
   a) Frolic in the forest, plant wheat an dig for clams
   b) Frolic in the forest, sow squash and dig for clams
   c) Frolic in the forest, sew dresses and plant squash and beans
   d) Frolic in the forest, sow squash and beans and eat clams

Chepi, Achiq's step mother was a kind women. Chepi's daughters were:
   a) Kind as well
   b) Sweet, smart and wise
   c) Wise and kind
   d) Not kind
   e) Difficult to be around

Why didn't Achiq go to the festival with her step-sisters?
   a) She was putting out a fire
   b) She was riding on a whale
   c) She was paying with the Moshup
   d) She was beading her necklace

Who is the magic that helps Achiq get to the festival?
   a) A fairy godmother
   b) A gnome
   c) A Nikommo
   d) Cinderella

How did Achiq get to the festival?
   a) On the back of a bob cat
   b) In a magic pumpkin coach
   c) On the back of a giant
   d) On the back of a whale

Rubric for ALL Constructed Response Questions

The constructed-response questions of the new 21st Century assessments ask students to produce his or her own answers to questions rather than selecting the correct response from a list. Some constructed-response questions require students to write short compositions – much like some of the questions in this unit. All constructed response questions can be corrected using the rubric below —quickly and easily – as long as we – the teachers – understand the content inside and out.

Remember what the objective of constructed response questions is:
"Constructed-response items for reading provide students with an opportunity to demonstrate basic understanding of passages and to reflect on what has been read in order to respond and create personal meaning. Constructed-response items also reinforce the concept of reading for a variety of reasons, especially to solve a problem or answer a question and learn about diverse perspectives, cultures and issues in traditional and contemporary literature."

Again, this rubric may be used for all constructed response questions in this handbook.

Rubric
Wow! Really, you carry around enough rubrics to use this with EACH question. Are you totally insane? No, no and no again. Just keep the number system in your head as you go through the questions.

Score	Description	Score Tally
4	Response answered the question, relates to the reading and student has a grasp of the main story element (s) applicable.	
3	Response answers the question, relates to the reading and student has a grasp of the main story element(s) applicable – but complete sentences were not used and there are problems with spelling and/or grammar.	
2	Response provides a partial answer with limited, incomplete or partially correct information	
1	Response is minimal or vague.	
0	No or incorrect response.	

Name: _____

Rubric for Constructed Response _____

Please attach assignment.

Score	Description	Score Tally
4	Response answered the question, relates to the reading and student has a grasp of the main story element (s) applicable.	
3	Response answers the question, relates to the reading and student has a grasp of the main story element(s) applicable – but complete sentences were not used and there are problems with spelling and/or grammar.	
2	Response provides a partial answer with limited, incomplete or partially correct information	
1	Response is minimal or vague.	
0	No or incorrect response.	

Teacher Comments: _____
_____
_____
_____
_____
_____

Student Comments: _____
_____
_____
_____
_____

I am thankful for...

Thanksgiving Science

Cranberry Chemistry—Spy Ink

Cranberries contain pigments called anthocyanins (an-tho-SY-a-nins). Anthocyanins give cranberries their bright color. The pigments make it easy for birds and other animals to fruit to see the fruit. This is extremely important because animals eat the berries and spread plants seeds from one place to another.

These pigments, called flavanoids, change color when they come in contact with acids an bases. Cranberry juice is very acidic, and the pigment is red in acids. When you add it to a base, it turns purple or blue.

Baking soda is a base, so your baking soda message will turn blue when it comes into contact with the pigments in the cranberry juice. Eventually, when enough cranberry juice soaks into the paper, it will dilute the baking soda and make the paper acidic, turning the pigment back to red and your message will disappear!

There are over 300 kinds of anthocyanins which are found in many fruits and vegetables including blueberries, red cabbage, grapes and blueberries. Scientists think they may have many health benefits and some researchers are even making organic solar cells using flavonoids!

You'll need
- half a bag of cranberries
- water
- baking soda
- printer paper works but construction paper works better because it is porous
- q-tips
- a homemade pen: *Cut the tip off of a q-tip at an angle and use the angle as a writing tool.*

Pre lesson: Boil the cranberries in 2 and ½ cups of water for 15 or 20 minutes. Crush the cooked berries and push the liquid through a sieve or colander to collect the concentrated cranberry juice.

Science Vocabulary:

Pigment: A pigment is a substance that gives color to something. **Great multimedia on pigment: http://mocomi.com/pigment/**

Anthocyanins: a pigment that gives fruits, plants and flowers their bright blue to red colors.

Bases: A base is a chemical compound that is bitter. Acids and bases are opposites
Characteristics:
Taste: bitter when dissolved in water
Touch: Feel Slippery

Acid: An acid is a chemical compound that is sour, like Sour Patch Kids.

Characteristics Acids are generally:
Taste: sour when dissolved in water

Cranberry Chemistry—Spy Ink

Mission: Write a secret message of Thanks that only your partner can read!

With cranberries and baking soda, you can create invisible messages that will be revealed to friendly eyes and self-destruct before your enemies have a chance to read them. You'll see how some pigments in fruit can change color when they're exposed to an acid or a base.

1. Pour cranberry juice into a baking dish or cake pan
2. Make Ink: add a few teaspoons of baking soda to ¼ cup of warm water and dissolve it. Don't worry if it doesn't dissolve completely.
3. Use your writing tool to write a message on your paper
4. Let your message dry. Or blow it with a blow dryer.
5. To reveal your message: submerge your paper in the cranberry juice

Enrichment: What other juices can you use to reveal secret messages? What else could you use as ink? If you use lemon juice as ink, does it turn a different color?

Question: _____

_____

_____

What is supposed to happen:	What I think will happen:

Cranberry Chemistry—Spy Ink

Write What Happened:

Illustrations:

Cranberry Chemistry—Spy Ink

Science Vocabulary

Turkey Glyphs

Objectives
Make a turkey glyph and guess which ones are your classmates.

Materials
Copies of turkey glyph cutouts - with lots of feathers
Colored construction paper
Color crayons, markers or colored pencils
1 copy of "Can You Find My Turkey"

Procedure
Cut, color and assemble turkey glyphs

Wait one day, then:

Display "Can you Find My Turkey" on the board
Hold up each turkey and have students guess - either orally or by writing them down in number sequence - who belongs to whose turkey.

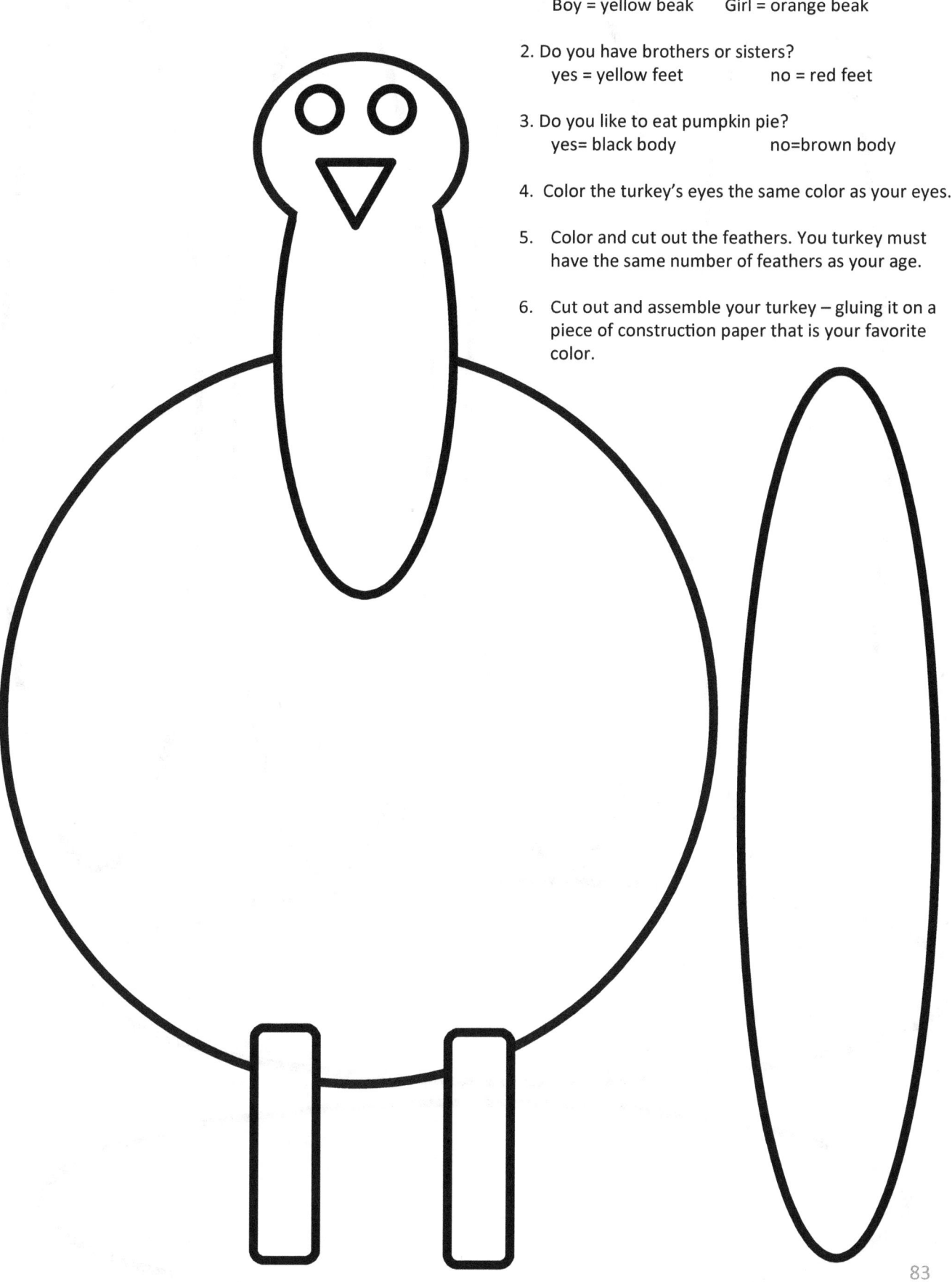

1. Are you a boy or a girl?
   Boy = yellow beak   Girl = orange beak

2. Do you have brothers or sisters?
   yes = yellow feet   no = red feet

3. Do you like to eat pumpkin pie?
   yes= black body   no=brown body

4. Color the turkey's eyes the same color as your eyes.

5. Color and cut out the feathers. You turkey must have the same number of feathers as your age.

6. Cut out and assemble your turkey – gluing it on a piece of construction paper that is your favorite color.

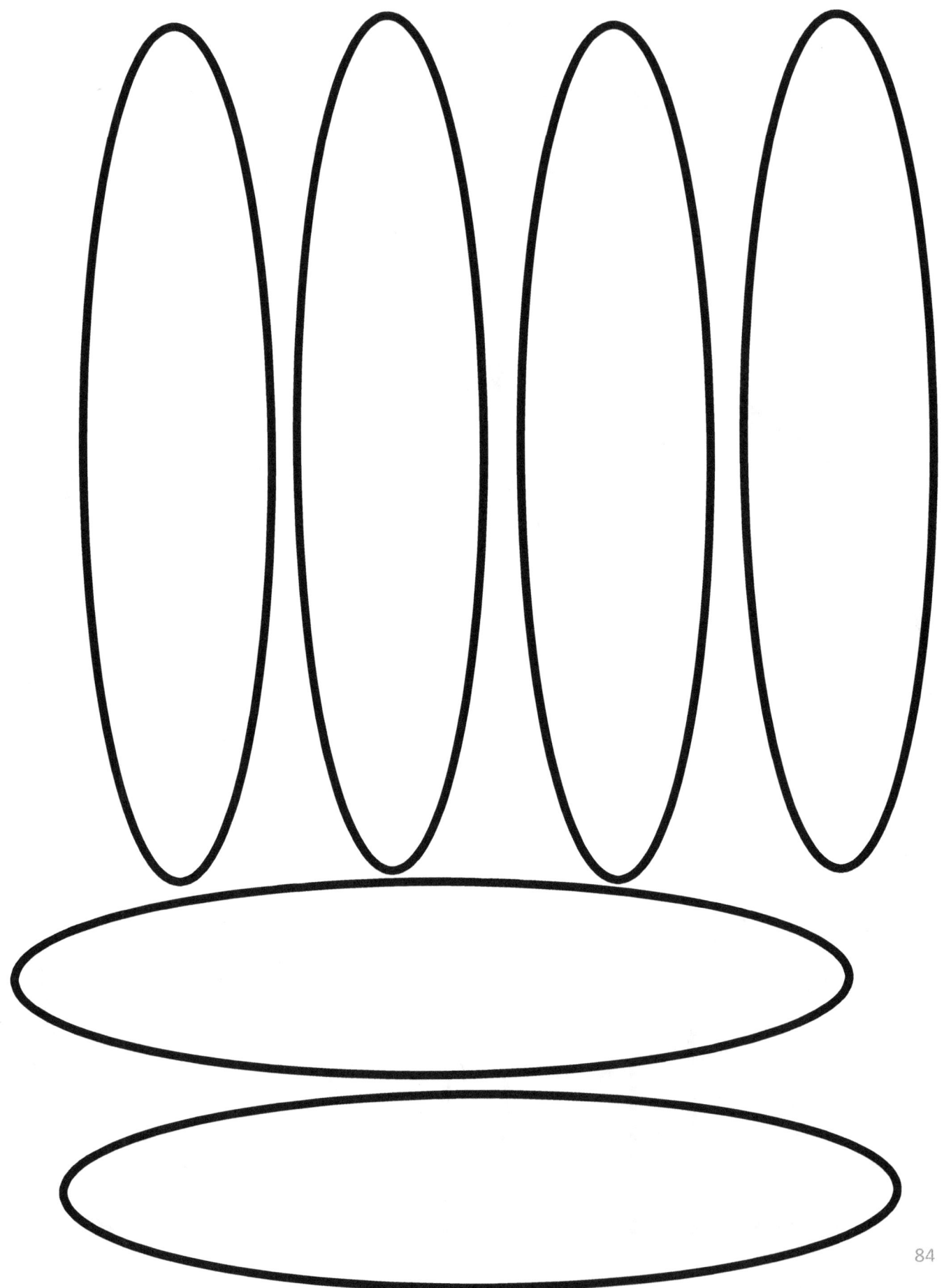

Turkey Glyphs

My name is _____ .

I am a _____ .

I _____ siblings.

My favorite color is _____ .

I _____ to eat pumpkin pie.

My eyes are _____ .

I am _____ years old.

Happy Fall!

Fall Art Projects
Leaf Pressing

Objectives
Students will collect and identify fall leaves.
Students will create art with ordinary objects.

Materials
Old phone books or encyclopedias
Collection of colorful fall leaves
Craft glue
White cardstock or watercolor paper

Procedure
Collect leaves.
Separate and place them between the pages of the books.

Have students use one page for each leaf and pacing them well apart from each other.

Place the books in a cool, dry place for a week to ten days. (Save the books and reuse them next year). A set or two of old encyclopedias are wonderful and there are always people who want to donate them.

Students then carefully apply craft glue to the back of the dried leaves and decorate pictures for either framing - or use construction paper and laminate them for Thanksgiving placements!

Corn Husk Dolls
http://www.snowwowl.com/naartcornhuskdolls2.html

Make a Mayflower
This one requires quite a bit of prep but is pretty cool:
http://artprojectsforkids.org/portfolio/make-a-mayflower-ship/

Turkey on a Stick
For a bit of math - print out the instructions and have students do this one all on their own.
http://artprojectsforkids.org/wp-content/uploads/2014/12/Recycle-Turkey-Diagram.pdf

Name: _____ Date: _____

#15 Veteran's Day

On November 11 of each year we celebrate Veteran Day, but when was this holiday first celebrated?

At 11:00 a.m. on November 11, 1910, World War I officially ended. The next year, November 11 was declared Armistice day by President Woodrow Wilson. Armistice means a formal agreement or truce. It was the President's intention to create a lasting peace after the war, so it was important to remember the peace agreement. He also wanted everyone to remember the sacrifices the military made for the United States and its allies during World War I.

In 1938, Congress declared November 11 a national holiday. When a town in Kansas organized a local Veterans Day Parade, a Kansas representative proposed a name change for the holiday. In 1954, President Eisenhower change the name from Armistice Day to Veterans Day.

As we celebrate Veterans Day and get ready to give thanks on Thanksgiving, it is important to remember all the brave men and women still serving out country.

Think and Write: On a separate piece of paper, please write a letter thanking a veteran. If you know one you may address it to him or her, if not, your teacher will collect them and send them to an organization that gets letters to veterans through your local American Legion.

Thank You!

_____

Dear Hero:

_____
_____
_____
_____
_____
_____
_____
_____
_____
_____
_____
_____
_____
_____

Sincerely,

_____

I am thankful
I am hopeful

According to the International Foundation for Research on Education and Depression (www.ifred.com) the main predictor of suicide isn't loneliness, life losses or trauma, it is hopelessness. Feelings of hopelessness have also been linked to the type of despair that enables children to act rashly and violently – often hurting themselves and/or others.

Helping students find hope and meaning in their lives, fostering connections and finding reasons to be thankful are difficult for many people, including our students. Feelings of hopelessness and disconnect can lead to depression, especially around the holidays, so as we talk about Thanksgiving and moving into the holiday season – it is a great time to help students and families find hope.

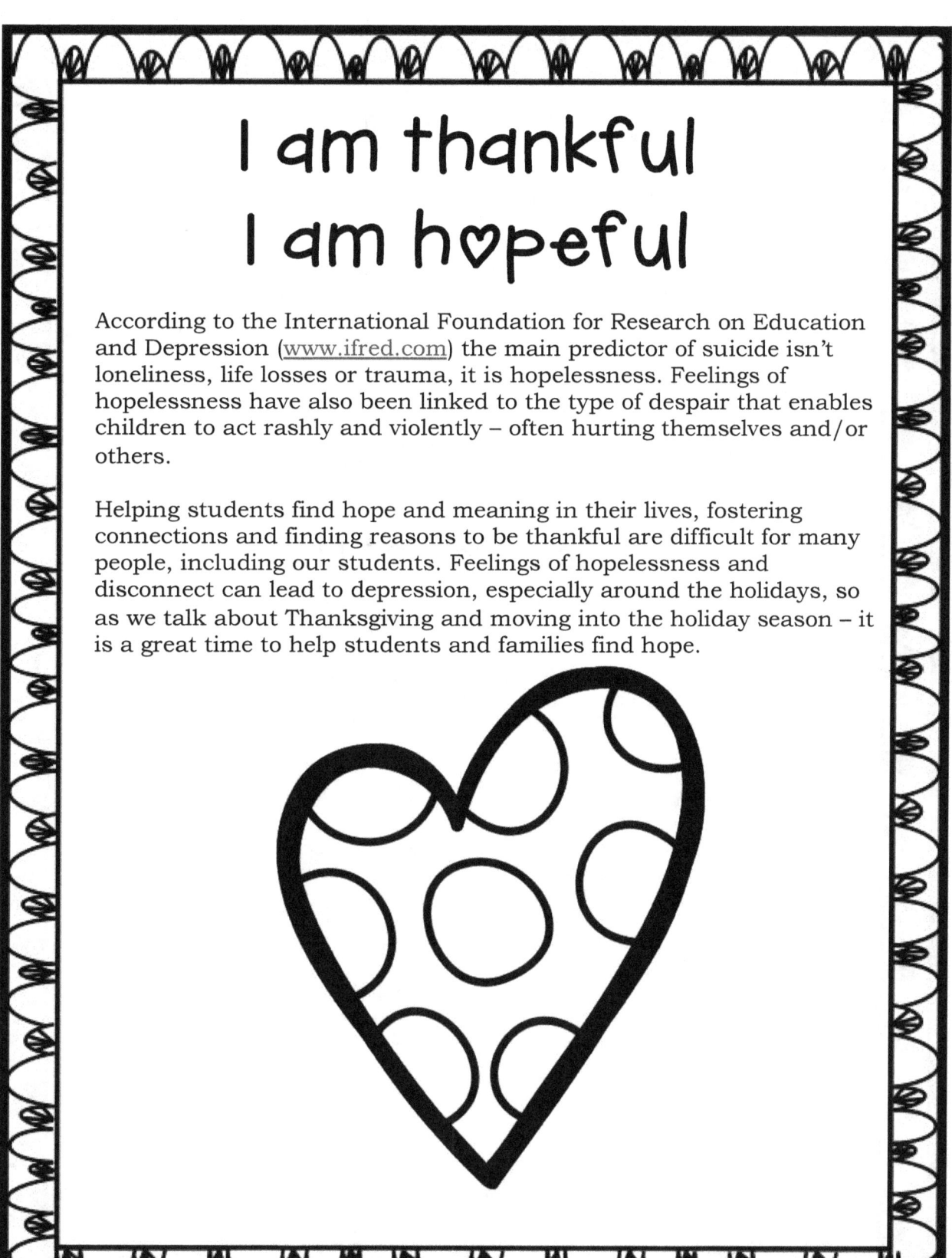

Our Patch of Hope

Objective: Build a Pumpkin Patch of Hope.

Instructions:
1. Copy the pumpkin leaf pattern onto green construction paper. One or two per student. Have students write what they are thankful for on each pumpkin leaf.
2. Copy the pumpkin leaf pattern onto white paper. Have students write what they are hopeful for, color their pumpkins.
3. Construct a bulletin board out of the pumpkin leaves.
4. Each day for five days leading up to Thanksgiving talk about being hopeful, what it means and share stories – see Pumpkin Patch Teacher's Notes.
5. After your discussion – have students cut and color one pumpkin – filling in what they are hopeful for and putting their pumpkins up on the bulletin board.

Our Patch of Hope Teacher Note Pages

1. Discuss what hope is. Hope is like swimming or playing a sport or reading – the more you swim or play football or read the better you get at these things. Hope is the same way. The more you practice your hope techniques the better they will become. But what does hope mean? (take suggestions)

    The feeling of wanting something to happen and believing it can

2. Summarize student definitions of hope, working it back to the bolded definition above and use that under the title for your **Pumpkin Patch of Hope**.

    Now talk about:
    - What is something that might or is going to happen soon that you are excited or hopeful for?
    - What is something that is going to happen next summer that you are hopeful for?
    - What can you think of that might happen this school year that you are hopeful for?
    - Close your eyes and think of a special person in your life that gives you hope.

3. Have students take a deep breath, close their eyes and visualize something they are hopeful for.

4. Begin building your **Pumpkin Patch of Hope**

5. Talk about hope each day, talk about how to decrease anxiety by taking deep breaths and being mindful of hope.

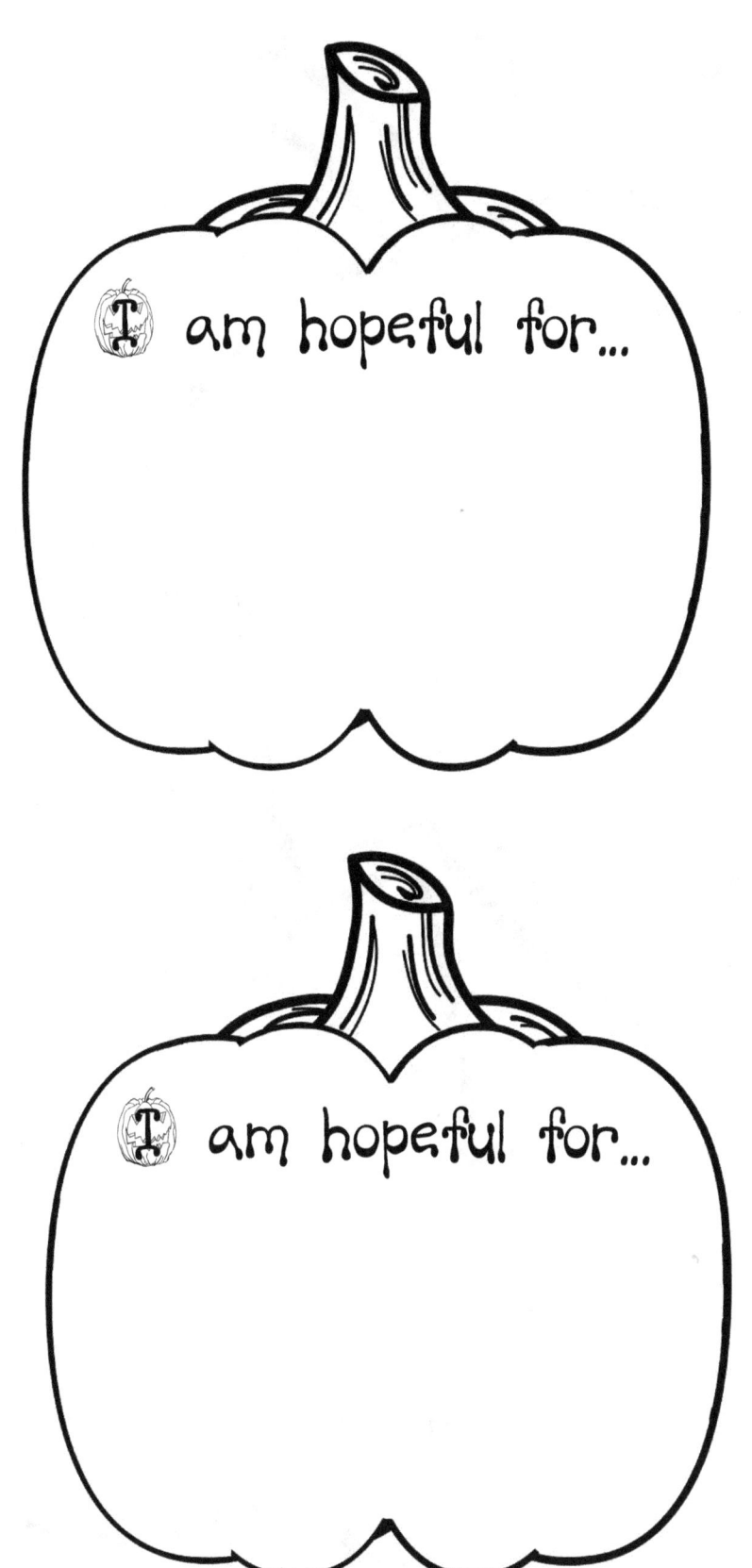

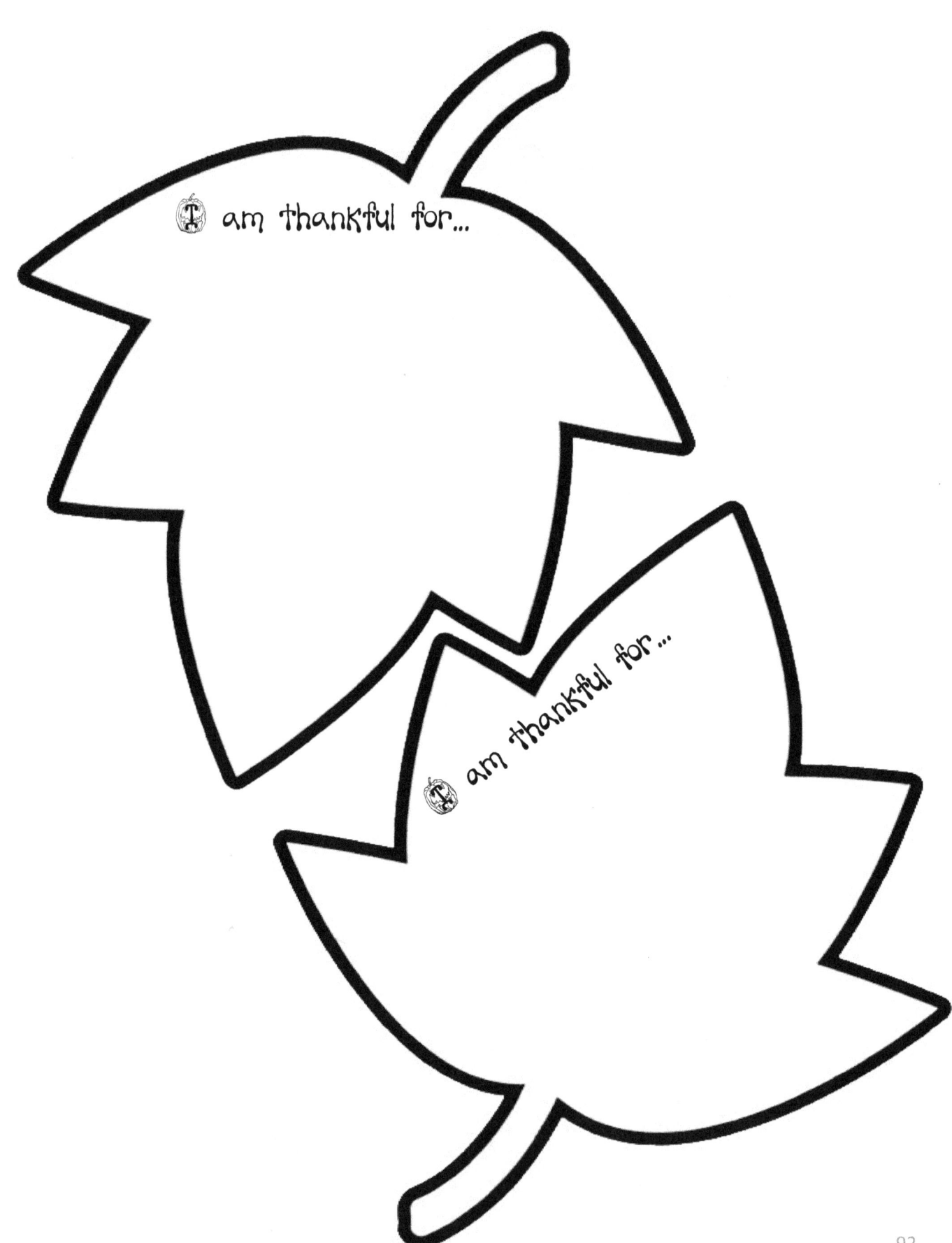

Thanksgiving Math

Hubbub

Log on to the internet and read:
https://www.plimoth.org/learn/just-kids/homework-help/fun-and-games

Then play: Hubbub

Materials: 5 flattish stones or bottle caps (for two sided dice); 50 popsicle sticks or toothpicks - counters; basket

Hubbub dice is a game of change played by the Wampanoag

The name hubbub evolved from the "hub, hub, hub" chant the colonists heard from the game's spectators. Today the word hubbub has come to define any boisterous activity. We don't know what the Wampanoag originally called the game.

1. Gather your materials
2. Decorate one side of each of the five two-sided "dice" you've chosen to use for the game. Draw stars on 3 of the dice, and x's on the other 2; leave the other side blank. Place the counters in a pile where they will be accessible to both players.
3. Begin play of hubbub dice by tossing the dice in the bowl. Take note of how many dice with stars.
4. Scoring:

Pattern Shown	Points
1 of either	0
2 x's	3
3 stars and 2 blanks	3
2 x's & 3 blanks	3
4 marked sides up	1
5 blank sides up	1
5 marked sides up	8

Task Card 1

1. William Brewster sailed from England to the shores of what is now New England on the Mayflower. He was in charge of packing the food. He had 859 potatoes that he had to divide between 33 people.

How many potatoes did each person receive?

2. Write your own Mayflower food word problem. Be sure to provide a solution.

Task Card 2

Humility worked hard planting crops for she and her fellow Pilgrims to eat. She divided her field into sections. She had 125 squash plants. If she plants an equal number of squash plants in each of 3 sections, how many plants will be in each section and how many plants will be left over.

Draw a squash and solve your problem inside the squash.

Task Card 3

The voyage from Plymouth, England to Plymouth Harbor is about **2,706 miles**, and took the Mayflower **66 days**. The Mayflower left England with **102** passengers.

1. If the Mayflower traveled an equal number of miles each day, how many miles did they travel in one day?
2. What information from the problem is not necessary to solve the problem?
3. Draw the Mayflower.

Task Card 4

The Wampanoag lived in wigwam-type houses. There were 110 wigwams in the largest village. If there are 330 people who live in the village, and everyone lived in one of the wigwams, list two different ways the Wampanoag can be spread out throughout the wigwams.

Task Card 5

The Wampanoag newlyweds, Achek and Annawan, spent their first year exploring the land west of their village.

They hiked 8 miles per day along a 125-mile-long trail. How many days will it take them to hike exactly 8 miles?

Solve and draw it out.

Task Card 6

The Mayflower left the Pilgrims and went back to England to get more supplies. The Pilgrims requested 1,252 blankets, to use and trade. Each shipping carton for the trip back could hold 8 blankets. How many cartons would be needed to ship all of the sleeping bags? Explain your answer.

Task Card 7

Fluency Builder. Solve the problems and explain the pattern.

1. 24 divided by 6
2. 240 divided by 6
3. 240 divided by 60

Task Card 8

1. Write a paragraph that involves the Pilgrims, the Mayflower and division.

2. Illustrate your problem.

Task Card 9

There were 12 children on the Mayflower. Each child had one pair of shoes and 2 coat. How many coats and shoes did they have in all?

5.OA.A2

Task Card 10

There were 12 children on the Mayflower. Each child had one pair of shoes and 2 coat. How many coats and shoes did they have in all?

5.OA.A2

Task Card 11

Write each phrase as a mathematical expression.

Phrase	Expression
The sum of five and seven	5 + 7
The sum of five and a number x	5 + x

The expression **5 + 7** represents a single number (17). This expression is a numerical expression. The expression **5 + x** represents a value that can change. If x is 2, then the expression **5 + x** has a value of 7. If x is 6, then the expression has a value of 11. So **5 + x** is an algebraic expression.

Phrase	Expression

5.OA.A2

Task Card 12

Write and algebraic expression for each phrase
5.OA.2

Phrase	Expression
Nine increased by a number x	
Ten decreased by a number p	
Seven less than a number t	
The product of 8 and a number n	
A number x increased by 25	
16 less than a number p	

Task Card 13

Write and algebraic expression:

The Mayflower company has $1000 to distribute to each person on the Mayflower as a bonus.

1. How much money will each employee get?

2. If there are 100 people left to get money. How much will each receive?

5.OA.2

Task Card 14

The Wampanoag share their wild apple orchard with Tom Pilgrim. If Tom Pilgrim picks 45 apples per hour and gives 20 of those apples back to the Wampanoag, how many apple will he have left after one day.

Write and algebraic expression letting x be the number of hours in a day.

5.OA.2

Task Card 15

Humility and Patience went to the shore to gather clams. Humility gathered 20 per hour and Patience gathered 16 per hour. If they worked for three hours, how many clams did they have in all?

Task Card 16

The Mayflower was 90 feet long and 26 feet wide. That is a pretty small boat, by today's standards, to be sailing across the ocean. The Mayflower could hold 180 "tuns" – a tun is a barrel that could hold 265 gallons of liquid.

1. Measure the length and width and determine if the Mayflower could fit in you classroom? How about in the library?

2. Bonus: using chalk and a long tape measure – measure and outline a rectangle the size of the Mayflower.

5.NTB.6

Task Card 17

There were 102 passengers on the Mayflower and 26 crew members. There were 50 men, 20 women and 32 children. One person died on the voyage and a baby boy was born.

1. How many more women and children than there were men?

2. How many more crew and children there were men?

Task Card 18

The Mayflower took 66 days to get to the shores of what is now New England.

How many weeks did they travel in all?

Task Card 1q

1. Twenty-one Native Americans lived in three wigwams. If the same number lived in each wigwam, how many were there in each?

2. There were twelve ducks and four hunters. If each hunter got and equal number of ducks, how many would each have?

Task Card 20

1. After 10 years living in their new land, each of 15 Pilgrim families had 4 children. How many children were there after 10 years?

2. There were 126 bushels of corn picked for each of 6 days. How many bushels of corn were there in all?

Task Card 1

1. William Brewster sailed from England to the shores of what is now New England on the Mayflower. He was in charge of packing the food. He had 825 potatoes that he had to divide between 25 people.

How many potatoes did each person receive? 33 each

2. Write your own Mayflower food word problem. Be sure to provide a solution.

Task Card 2

Humility worked hard planting crops for she and her fellow Pilgrims to eat. She divided her field into sections. She had 125 squash plants. If she plants an equal number of squash plants in each of 3 sections, how many plants will be in each section and how many plants will be left over.

Draw a squash and solve your problem inside the squash.

Each section has 41 plants and there are two plants left over.

Task Card 3

The voyage from Plymouth, England to Plymouth Harbor is about **2,706 miles**, and took the Mayflower **66 days**. The Mayflower left England with **102** passengers.

1. If the Mayflower traveled an equal number of miles each day, how many miles did they travel in one day? They traveled 41 miles per day.
2. What information from the problem is not necessary to solve the problem? 102 passengers
3. Draw the Mayflower.

Task Card 4

The Wampanoag lived in wigwam-type houses. There were 110 wigwams in the largest village. If there are 330 people who live in the village, and everyone lived in one of the wigwams, list two different ways the Wampanoag can be spread out throughout the wigwams.

1. 3 people living in each wigwam
2. 2 people living in 75 wigwams, 4 people living in 30, 12 people living in 4 and 12 crowded into 1

Answers may vary

Task Card 5

The Wampanoag newlyweds, Achek and Annawan, spent their first year exploring the land west of their village.

They hiked 8 miles per day along a 125-mile-long trail. How many days will it take them to hike exactly 8 miles?

Solve and draw it out.

Answer: 15 days

Task Card 6

The Mayflower left the Pilgrims and went back to England to get more supplies. The Pilgrims requested 1,252 blankets, to use and trade. Each shipping carton for the trip back could hold 8 blankets. How many cartons would be needed to ship all of the sleeping bags? Explain your answer.

157 cartons would be needed because 1,252, divided by 8 blankets equals 156 with 4 left over. That means there would have to be 157 shipping cartons

Task Card 7

Fluency Builder. Solve the problems and explain the pattern.

1. 24 divided by 6   4
2. 240 divided by 6   40
3. 240 divided by 60   4

When you add a zero to one, you get a zero in the solution, but when you add a zero to both they cancel each other out.

Task Card 8

1. Write a paragraph that involves the Pilgrims, the Mayflower and division.

2. Illustrate your problem.

Answers will vary

Task Card 9

There were 12 children on the Mayflower. Each child had one pair of shoes and 2 coat. How many coats and shoes did they have in all?

Answer: 12 x 2 shoes = 24
2 x (24 + 12)
2 x (36) = 72

5.OA.A2

Task Card 10

There were 12 children on the Mayflower. Each child had one pair of shoes and 2 coat. How many coats and shoes did they have in all?

Answer: 12 x 2 shoes = 24
2 x (24 + 12)
2 x (36) = 72

5.OA.A2

Task Card 11

Write each phrase as a mathematical expression.

Phrase	Expression
The sum of five and seven	5 + 7
The sum of five and a number x	5 + x

The expression **5 + 7** represents a single number (17). This expression is a numerical expression. The expression **5 + x** represents a value that can change. If x is 2, then the expression **5 + x** has a value of 7. If x is 6, then the expression has a value of 11. So **5 + x** is an algebraic expression.

Phrase	Expression

5.OA.A2

Task Card 12

Write and algebraic expression for each phrase
5.OA.2

Phrase	Expression
Nine increased by a number x	9 + x
Ten decreased by a number p	10 - p
Seven less than a number t	t - 7
The product of 8 and a number n	8n
A number x increased by 25	25 + x
16 less than a number p	p - 16

Task Card 13

Write and algebraic expression:

The Mayflower company has $1000 to distribute to each person on the Mayflower as a bonus.

1. How much money will each employee get?

Answer: 1000/x

2. If there are 100 people left to get money. How much will each receive?

1000 divided by 100 equals 10 dollars each. They will each receive 10 dollars

5.OA.2

Task Card 14

The Wampanoag share their wild apple orchard with Tom Pilgrim. If Tom Pilgrim picks 45 apples per hour and gives 20 of those apples back to the Wampanoag, how many apple will he have left after one day.

Write and algebraic expression letting x be the number of hours in a day.

Answer: 45x – 20

5.OA.2

Task Card 15

Humility and Patience went to the shore to gather clams. Humility gathered 20 per hour and Patience gathered 16 per hour. If they worked for three hours, how many clams did they have in all?

Answer: 3 (16 + 20)
16 clams for Patience plus 20 for Humility = 36 clams

They gathered 36 clams per hour for three hours
36 x 3 = 108

Task Card 16

The Mayflower was 90 feet long and 26 feet wide. That is a pretty small boat, by today's standards, to be sailing across the ocean. The Mayflower could hold 180 "tuns" – a tun is a barrel that could hold 265 gallons of liquid.

1. Measure the length and width and determine if the Mayflower could fit in you classroom? How about in the library?

2. Bonus: using chalk and a long tape measure – measure and outline a rectangle the size of the Mayflower.

5.NTB.6

Task Card 17

There were 102 passengers on the Mayflower and 26 crew members. There were 50 men, 20 women and 32 children. One person died on the voyage and a baby boy was born.

1. How many more women and children than there were men? $20 + 32 - 50 = 2$ more women and children

2. How many more crew and children there were men? $32 + 26 - 50 = 7$ more children and crew

Task Card 18

The Mayflower took 66 days to get to the shores of what is now New England.

How many weeks did they travel in all?

66 divided by 7 = 9 weeks with a remainder of three so 10 weeks.

Task Card 19

1. Twenty-one Native Americans lived in three wigwams. If the same number lived in each wigwam, how many were there in each?

21 divided by 3 = 7 in each wigwam

2. There were twelve ducks and four hunters. If each hunter got and equal number of ducks, how many would each have?

12 divided by 4 = 3

Task Card 20

1. After 10 years living in their new land, each of 15 Pilgrim families had 4 children. How many children were there after 10 years?

Answer: 15 families x 4 children = 60 children

2. There were 126 bushels of corn picked for each of 6 days. How many bushels of corn were there in all?

Answer: 126 x 6 756 bushels in all

Task Card